The Liverpool Windjammers

Volume One

John Richardson

A Countyvise Publication

Front and back cover of this book portray the full rigged ship *Liverpool*. At the timc of her Glasgow launch in 1889, the masted *Liverpool* was the largest merchant sailing ship in the world.

First Published 2006 by Countyvise Limited,
14 Appin Road, Birkenhead, Wirral CH41 9HH.

British Library Cataloguing in Publication Data.
A catalogue record for this book is available from the British Library.

Please note: From 1st January 2007 ISBNs will contain 13 numbers these numbers will be the same as the present number printed below the barcode (ie. starting 978).
Countyvise is showing both existing (10 digit) and future (13 digit) ISBNs on the Title page verso. Please continue to use the 10 figure number until 31st December 2006.

ISBN 1 901231 70 4 ISBN 978 1 901231 70 0

For

Angela and Darren

Contents

Ilustrations

Page

Captain Keith Meyer of the South African Navy

Captain Keith Meyer who has helped the author in the writing of this book, stands before a painting of the South African Training Ship '*General Botha'*, a ship that once served in the same capacity as the British *'Vindicatrix'*. The oil painting was commissioned by Captain Meyer, who on its completion by the author, presented it to the 'General Botha Old Boys Association.'

As a ship, the *General Botha* was originally the British light cruiser HMS Thames of 1886. After thirty-four years' service in the Royal Navy, she arrived at Cape Town in 1921 to begin the second stage of her career, this being as a training ship for boys who later joined various shipping companies as midshipmen, cadets or lower deck ratings.

After having had so many trainees tread her decks, to follow the time honoured rituals of holystoning, chipping and scraping, as well as the many other tasks that befall a boy to make him a man, the SATS *General Botha* eventually reverted to her original name in 1942. Then with great ceremony in 1947 whilst in the third and final stage of her career, she was used as a target in Simons Bay.

Prior to becoming an apprentice in the ships of the South African Railways and Harbour Administration, Captain Meyer attended the 'New' General Botha, a shore establishment at Granger Bay in Cape Town. At the time of writing, Captain Meyer is the president of The General Botha Old Boy's Association.

Foreword

In my experience of the maritime world, I consider myself most fortunate in being acquainted with the author of the 'Liverpool Windjammers.' My interest in ships of sail began during the years of my apprenticeship, those unforgettable years when I was serving in the South African coal burners *Dalia* and *Alloe.* On my frequent visits to Lourenco Marques, the stately *Lawhill* could be seen laid up awaiting disposal for quite some time. How sad it was to see the passing away of such a lovely ship, for the world shall never see her like again. However, there are those amongst us who have the ability to retain such beauty on canvas, and indeed the author is one of them. Furthermore, due to his British Merchant Navy background, he is in every sense a seaman. 'The Liverpool Windjammers' is a publication of great importance, both for the history of Liverpool and those enthusiasts of sailing ships the world over. In reading through the manuscript my mind wandered back to the words of Masefield when he wrote '*I must go down to the sea again, to the lonely sea and sky, and all I ask is a tall ship and a star to steer her by.'* There were other classics like the words of Gilbert and Sullivan. *"To lay aloft in a howling gale may tickle a landsman's taste ....* all of which, puts me in mind of the bitterly hard times endured by those sailors - so clearly described within these pages. It is a well known fact that with the introduction of steamships in the nineteenth century, a great rivalry developed between the seamen of the steamers, and the sailors of the clippers; they were different breeds and worlds apart. The steamer seamen would refer to their sailing vessel counterparts as 'windjammers' - ships and men, who due to their inability to sail close to the wind, had to be 'jammed' into it with their yards braced hard over on the backstays. In their reply, the sailors claimed that whereas the smoke belching steamers prayed for a rising barometer, mild seas and blue skies, the real sailors sought low pressures and howling gales for their fast passages.

For its power of description and clarity, 'The Liverpool Windjammers' is commended for bringing back an era so lamentably lost, and as to its author, who has added yet another chapter to Liverpool's great maritime past, he deserves every credit for his efforts.

Captain Keith Meyer (South African Navy Rtd.)

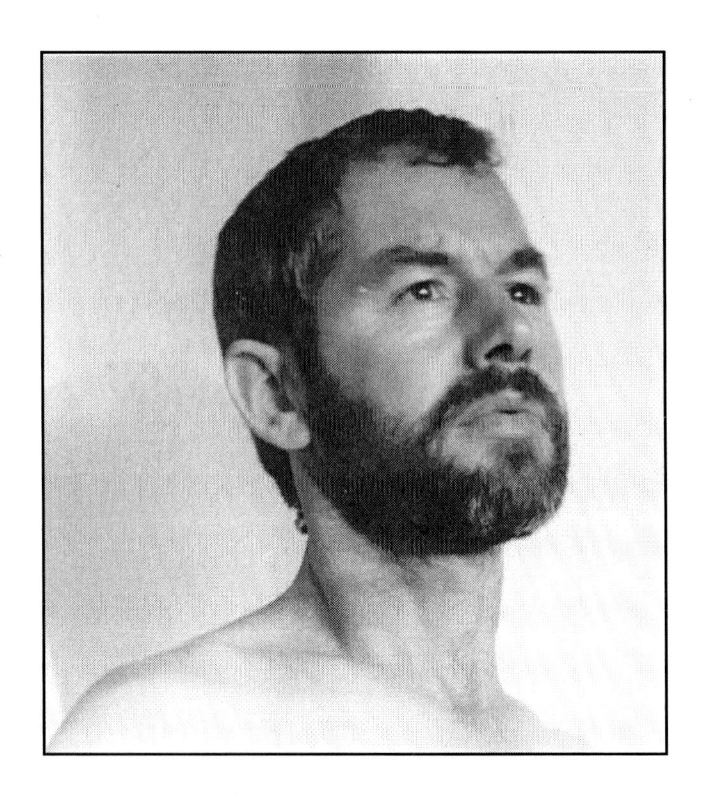

About the Author

John Richardson was born in Liverpool in 1937. On joining the Sea Cadets in 1950, he spent two years at a Nautical School before joining the Merchant Navy in 1953. It was on his first ship the *Willesden* of London, that he started on the long and arduous road of becoming a marine artist. It was also a ship on which he kept a record of daily events, thus resulting in his first book 'A Deck Boy's Diary.'

After serving aboard various types of ships until 1990 he continued with his art, but on his retirement from the sea began writing about his paintings, which in the main were ships of sail. Married in 1963 he lives with his wife and two sons in Wiltshire. His eldest son became a government official after he had served in the Army, whilst the youngest is a master mariner.

Introduction

As the elegant clipper ships began their departure from the seas and into the history books, a new breed of ocean carrier arrived to take their place. These replacements were built of iron or steel, but quite unlike the clipper ships before them, their box-like bows left little in the way of underwater lines. They were in general much larger though rather slower than the more stylish clippers; however, they were turned out much faster.
The sceptics of the day who were the sailors themselves, said that the new style of sailing vessels were built by the mile then sawn off into lengths. They were said to be ugly, undermanned and hungry, furthermore, those same sailors referred to them as floating workhouses. Indeed, those very ships were the ones that were to be termed as the 'windjammers.' Although the name of 'windjammer' is not a recognised sailing vessel rig, the slang term was in general applied to the latest ocean going sailing ships of the 19th century. It would appear therefore, that from then on and right up to the present day, any sail powered vessel or sail assisted steamer might be referred to as being a windjammer.
Up to and including the 18th century, any alterations in the building of ships and their rigs was so slow, that any change which did come about was hardly noticeable. Indeed, it was difficult to tell the difference between one ship built in 1699, and another with the same tonnage of 1799. However, and as the 19th century evolved, shipbuilding underwent many radical changes, and indeed, the introduction of iron into the shipyards played a major role. Furthermore, from those times on it wasn't just the ship's hulls, masts and yards that were being built of iron, another important addition was the manufacture of iron wire rope, then at a later date steel wire rope.
Those cumbersome lower shrouds and backstays which since the early times had supported ship's masts on outside channels, could then be replaced by the modern wire ropes. Furthermore, as well as being less in circumference than natural fibre ropes, this new innovation had a number of other advantages. The wire ropes were inch for inch much stronger, required less maintenance, and were much less prone to stretching. This latter fact in itself, was greatly responsible for reducing the time consuming and never ending job of setting up the rigging. Although iron wire rope had been used in various forms for some time, hawser laid wire rope as we know it today was the invention of the German mining engineer Wilhelm Albert. He'd been experimenting with it for some years before manufacturing it into lengths of 25 fathoms, and with the additional innovation of

the wire long splice, any number of these manufactured lengths could be joined together.
The original concept of wire ropes was for use in the German coal mines, where at the pit shaft they enabled coal to be hauled to the surface much more efficiently. During those times, coal from the coal-face was usually transported in carts by ponies on narrow gauge tracks to the pit shaft. Many years later, the pit ponies were dispensed with and an endless haulage system was employed. The endless haulage rope consisted of a number of 120 fathom coils of flexible steel wire rope, these coils were joined together *en situ*, with long splices by the mine riggers. The endless rope which was often a number of miles long, would lead from a winch barrel at the pit shaft, past a series of sheaves until it reached the coal-face - then back to the pit shaft. The wire rope of the endless haulage system would be constantly on the move unless it was stopped for the connecting or releasing of the coal carts.
The wire rope of Wilhelm Albert was introduced to the world in 1834, and although it was quickly employed in the mining industry of Germany, it was some time before ship owners and their builders put the concept to full use. The ***SS Great Britain*** of 1843 was one of the earliest ships to use iron wire for its standing rigging. As for the rest of the deep water ships, the 1850s saw the gradual disappearance of the natural fibre ropes as standing rigging. At the same time, the outside channels which doubtless took a certain amount of speed off ships that used them also made a slow disappearance. It would appear therefore, that the introduction of the iron wire ropes reduced much of the sailor's workload. This was combined with the ending of the tea monopoly in 1834, which in turn, signalled the beginning of drastically reduced crews on all ships of sail.
The concept of steamships had been in existence from about 1790, a time when all sea going vessels were sail powered. However, just 100 years later at the end of the 19th century, the majority of ships were steamers. Therefore, it was during this one hundred year period that the transition from sail to steam was made. Although steamers had taken a firm grip on the world's maritime commerce before the end of the 19th century, sailing vessels of all shapes and sizes were still being churned out in the windjammer boom; a programme that reached its height between 1880 and 1890.
Of this new style of sailing vessel, and from the ship owner's point of view, it would appear that the steel four masted barque was the most economical in the deep sea trade. Indeed, with these huge ocean carriers, ship owners were able to use ever smaller crews. After the four masted barques in popularity came the bald headers and the three masted barques, then the iron and steel full rigged ships. To the sailors who manned these vessels they were absolute workhouses. It wasn't so much because of the hard and dangerous work that made those ships so life threatening, but because in so many cases the ships were undermanned. The food allowance which as well as being poor in the first place, was on many ships scaled right down to the starvation rations of the Board of Trade scale, yet how many times have we heard - or read! of one particular ship that has made enough

profit from one voyage to pay for all her building costs?
However, legislation was eventually and reluctantly passed by the British government to safeguard the seamen. The new rules were made to ensure that every ship was fully manned, as well as giving the sailor enough food to sustain his health and well being. Unfortunately, and in some cases, those rules were hardly worth the paper they were written on, because when a ship did put to sea another set of rules often appeared. These might be used by the ship's master who could in fact sail as short handed as he thought fit, because in the cleverly worded rules and laws made by the Board of Trade, there were also little clauses that read, 'in certain circumstances' such as when it is impossible to sign men on to make up the full complement, or when food can not be obtained in reasonable circumstances, then the ship's master may use his own discretion.
Before the advent of iron and steel into the shipyards, there were the ships of the East India Company. Those vessels were hardly built for speed, and a voyage of two years or more to the Far East and back to the UK was in keeping with the times. Nevertheless, those ships were well thought of by their large crews of sailors, because when they were outward or homeward bound to or from the east, they would invariably stop off at Durban, Cape Town, St. Helena or Madeira for fresh fruit and vegetables. Whilst at sea and especially if the weather was threatening, sail would be reduced to a minimum; the apple-cheeked ship would then snug down and ride the weather out. Some ship's captains would even reduce sail before darkness with no threat of bad weather, even sending the t'gallant masts down each evening just to be on the safe side ... or often as a seamanship exercise. Those were the times when nobody was in a hurry, and also a time when there was an abundance of sailors on every ship.
But by the time the windjammers arrived things had changed drastically. The tea monopoly had gone as had the clippers, iron and steel had come and ship's crews were reduced to the absolute minimum. Labour was not so cheap anymore, and cargo ships seldom if ever stopped for fresh food and water whilst on passage.
After the demise of the East Indiaman the race was on, and in order to arrive at a loading or discharging port in record time, many a captain would risk his own life as well as that of his crew and ship. Even after having been at sea for many weeks, and perhaps with Table Mountain visible in its passing, the big jute windjammers didn't call in at Cape Town for fresh food and water anymore. The equally large ships on passage to or from San Francisco also passed many places where they could have re-provisioned.
A common practice to replenish food supplies at sea was to catch fish, sharks and seabirds, and on just about every ship that went to sea those methods were employed. Amongst sailors it has always been believed to be a bad omen to kill an albatross, but superstitions are set aside when survival is the first rule of life. Indeed, many an albatross

and other seabirds ended their existence on the galley stove. Fresh water has always been the most valued of provisions on any sailing ship, at all times sparingly doled out for drinking only. Although crews normally had enough to drink, there was never any left for dhobying. The Board of Trade scale was four quarts per man - per day - perhaps! Half of which went to the galley. Indeed, on that commodity there was never any wastage. Whenever a deluge of rain was experienced at sea, it was often the practice to spread a rain sail to catch as much water as possible, it then enabled the water tanks or barrels to be somewhat replenished. Tropical rainstorms were always welcome, it was the only time a seafarer could have a decent wash.

Since the clipper ship days, ships were being built bigger and bigger, whilst the crews to man them were becoming smaller and smaller. In order to evaluate just how some of those ships had been allowed to become so poorly manned, and with no apparent hard and fast legislation, it may be worth making comparisons between ships of various times.

The East Indiaman *Earl of Balcarres* was built in 1815, she had a tonnage of some 1,400 tons and was a big ship for her day. As well as her officers and midshipmen, plus whatever stewards she carried, there were also 78 sailors in her complement. No doubt many of these were gunners as well as sailors, because pirates were abundant in the China Seas. Nevertheless, there was always an abundance of seamen on each of the company's many ships.

The *Superb* of 1866 was a similar sized ship of 1,450 tons ... with no guns! She had 24 able seamen and a host of midshipmen and boys. Another of the company's ships was the little *Anglesey* of 1,018 tons built in 1851, she carried 22 on deck as well as the usual boys and midshipmen. Then in the 1850s there were the Liverpool Yankee Clippers, the fastest merchant sailing ships the world had ever seen; at some 2,000 tons, these ships each carried 48 sailors.

In comparison with those vessels mentioned, there were many ships like the ***Wavertree*** and ***Lawhill***, ships that sailed in the 1890s, and ships that were both over 2,000 tons. By then however, a marked difference in crew numbers was clearly visible, for these two vessels only carried 16 sailors each, a figure that included four to eight apprentices. Even the mighty *Liverpool* of 3,400 tons, the largest merchant sailing ship in the world, only had room in her foc'sle for 22 seamen, a figure that included her half dozen or so apprentices.

Furthermore, when she was trading in her early years, the ***Cutty Sark*** carried a complement of over 30 hands. However, by the time she was sold to the Portuguese and re-named ***Ferreira*** in 1895, her total crew was reduced to 20. Then when cut down to a barquentine at Cape Town in 1918, her total crew numbered just 12.

There were hundreds of shipping companies large and small, and of these, there was only a small portion that treated their sailors well. Many ships if not most were so mean and hungry, that their owners specifically hired captains who needed no telling on how to ill treat their men ... or to sail as shorthanded as possible. Moreover, it was their common practice to replace worn sails and tattered rigging as a last resort only. Some people will say that on the demise of the Blackwall Frigates, when ships were better manned and life at sea more leisurely, seamanship skills began a long decline which has lasted right up to the present day.

There are also those who say that iron ships and wire rope created a new type of sailor. Indeed, it is true that those who were able to splice wire rope were highly regarded. Those men usually came from rigging lofts, and their skills with the spike was always a well kept secret. Then there was the innovation of the unpopular chipping hammer and scraper, items that were to become the mode for all the steel built ships of both sail and steam.

Contrary to general belief, and although the wage of an able seaman was a pitiful 2/- a day or £3 a month .... for a minimum working day of 14 hours, that figure was a good wage in the 1890s in comparison with the rest of the working class. In fact, many seamen who'd been unable to spend their earnings due to a long passage, often paid off with a sizeable amount. It must also pointed out, that our forebears of the nineteenth century enjoyed an entirely different lifestyle than we do today.

Times were hard for everybody, business just as competitive, and heavily taxed ship owners had to keep an eye on every penny. Employers of the day were often referred to as being oppressive and mean, but their actions were all in keeping with the times ... and as far as business was concerned, only the strong survived! Indeed, without those so called oppressive employers of yesteryear, and the so called cruel captains who had to maintain strict discipline with some most unruly crews, what would the masses have done for employment?

The following pages will describe some of the ships and the men who sailed those ships at the end of the windjammer era. It will also tell of the extreme hardships suffered by the seamen of the day, when every person on board from the captain down to the boy had to be a sailor. Through countless hours of research, every effort has been made to obtain true facts for this publication. Although its drawings and colour plates mostly originate from builder's plans, it must be explained that some of the ships portrayed within, often underwent radical appearance changes during their careers; there were also a number that changed ownership with or without name changes.

For these reasons, many ships differed in appearance from time to time. Some of the facts in this manuscript may have been written by people before me, and whereas it is not the intention of the author to re-write what has already been written by others - history cannot change - the main object of this book is to describe a particular ship, present its picture and make further compilations. Much of the contents of these writings have been supplied to me by individuals whose forebears have actually served under sail, from correspondents, and also from information supplied to me by some of my own shipmates who have served before the mast.

With regard to the descriptions of the ships within these pages, the length of a vessel is at all times given as being between perpendiculars! This length abbreviated as 'bp' is measured from the rabbet at the inside of the stem on the main deck, to the inside of the stern frame on the same deck. It does not therefore include the overhang of the stem or stern, and neither does it include the bowsprit or jib-boom. Furthermore, all measurements are given in imperial sizes or nautical, just as they were in the days of the windjammer.

A glossary has been included at the end of the book.

John Richardson

Cape Town! A city which lies beneath Table Mountain, and one where it was once a common sight to see a forest of sailing ship masts in Table Bay.

Photo by the author

Arranmore

Whereas the object of 'The Liverpool Windjammers' is to identify a number of Liverpool registered sailing vessels, a few exceptions have been made with one ship in particular named *Arranmore* being purposefully described. The inclusion of this former Cape Horner is meant as a compliment to the men of the British Merchant Navy, for this was the very ship which later became the *Vindicatrix.* Indeed, a ship that laid the foundations for many young men who made the British Merchant Navy their career.

Photo—James Maguire

This impressive photograph of the *Arranmore* was taken at San Francisco between 1905 and 1910. The *Arranmore* was known as being a bald header, this relatively new innovation to sailing ship's rigs, meant there were no royal sails above the split topgallants. The ship was very powerfully rigged, and if the 24 foot lifeboats can be taken as a guide, then the huge mast doublings must have been of equal length. Also shown is the chartroom on the poop deck, the galley abaft the foremast and the gig boat on its roof. The portholes indicate her sailors were probably accommodated under the foc'sle head. On the after end of the foc'sle the white painted port lighthouse can be seen; a fish tackle used for hauling in the anchor is also prominent.

During their existence at Port Glasgow, Russell's Ship Yard had built many ships of both steam and sail. However, when one of their 1893 products took to the water, they could hardly have visualised the future this vessel was to have. That ship was the ***Arranmore*** which began her maritime career for the Sailing Ship Arranmore Co Ltd. This firm was managed by Thomson & Dickie's Maiden City Line of Glasgow. Launched in 1893 she was a sister to the ***Largiemore,*** built in the previous year for the same owners. The ***Arranmore*** whose signal letters were NFJV, was 1,946 gross and 1,794 nett tons, her sister was just eight gross tons smaller. These two steel ships were the largest under Thomson & Dickie's ownership.
The dimensions of these two ships were 263.8 x 39 x 23.6. Both these vessels were noted for their heavy rig, the lower yards on the fore and main masts being 90 feet in length. Therefore, with the ship's beam being 39 feet, it meant that those lower yards protruded by more than 25 feet over the ship's side when the yards were squared. Although these two vessels came from the same plan and were sister ships, their appearance differed greatly in their rig. ***Arranmore*** was stump t'gallant or bald headed, whilst the ***Largiemore*** had royals on all three masts.
The ***Arranmore*** began her maiden voyage shortly after being launched in October 1893. Captain Thompson her first commander, was one who had been unfortunate in losing his previous ship the ***Templemore.*** This was another of Thomson & Dickie's ships, and one that sank after colliding with an iceberg south of the Falklands in 1892.
After a sea career which spanned almost 50 years, the ***Arranmore*** was to be Captain Thompson's last command. Staying in the ship for six years until retiring from the sea in 1899, he settled in his native Stromness. It was there that he had a villa called Arranmore built, fittingly named after his last ship.
Captain Caw then took command of the ***Arranmore***. He was yet another captain who'd lost his last ship, this time it was the ***Blairmore***, a vessel also owned by Thomson & Dickie. That ship had capsized in Mission Bay San Francisco. It was whilst the ship lay at anchor in ballast waiting to load a cargo of grain, that in a sudden squall hit the wall sided ship and she went over. At the time of her capsizing, the second mate, the apprentices and a number of sailors were working in the hold and quite unable to escape; many of them drowned.
When Captain Caw joined the ***Arranmore*** she sailed to Portland for a cargo of grain. Regrettably, Captain Caw became ill during the passage; he was landed ashore at Antofagasta where at the local hospital he later died of his illness. Mr Howes the first mate then assumed command and the ship continued her passage to Portland. Captain Howes remained as master, and on the ship's return to the UK he brought his wife aboard for the following voyage. On this trip the ship sailed once again to Portland where yet another

cargo of wheat was loaded into her hold. The ship's destination was Algoa Bay in South Africa, where the ship which was then 10 years old arrived on 8 September 1903. However, there were no port facilities at Algoa Bay, and all visiting ships had to load and discharge at their moorings. After nine weeks of pleasant weather, and during which time the wheat cargo had been discharged, and 1,200 tons of sand ballast loaded, the ***Arranmore*** was almost ready for sea.

A large number of ships were also at the anchorage, these included steam, sail and a number of cargo lighters. However, the weather suddenly sprang up during the night of 13 November 1903. In the ensuing high winds and heavy seas, the ***Arranmore*** - through no fault of her own, was in collision with the SS ***Mashona.***

It later transpired that during the hours of darkness, the ***Mashona*** had attempted to steam out of the bay to the safety of the open sea. But in doing so, she collided with the ***Arranmore*** by fouling her anchor cables. This resulted in the sailing vessel being torn from her moorings. As she struck the beach the ***Arranmore*** lost her fore and main masts, with only the mizzen lower mast left standing.

Inchcape Rock

Built for the Cornfoot Line of Glasgow, The full rigged ship *Inchcape Rock* was blown ashore at Algoa Bay after the great storm of 1903. Although in the above photo she looks as though she could be salved, the damage to her underwater hull was too severe. A resultant survey declared her as being a total loss.

Sayre

Yet another stranding casualty of the great Algoa Bay storm.

Photos - South African Archives

Algoa Bay After the Great Storm of 1903

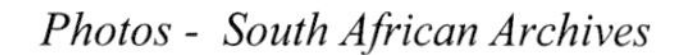

Photos - South African Archives

Just four of the victims blown ashore were the *Emmanuel, Iris, Oakworth* and *Constant.* Further up the beach there was so much wreckage from so many ships, all piled up in a mountain, it was impossible to tell from which ship the pieces of wreckage belonged.

Previous to the *Arranmore's* grounding, another storm of great proportions had taken place at the same anchorage which involved the *Wavertree and is* later described in volume Two.

In the collision which rendered the ship completely helpless, the crew as well as the captain's wife and child were fortunate enough to escape the catastrophe; in doing so they were able to climb over the tangled masts and rigging which formed a bridge to the shore. At a later date an inquiry was held into the ship's stranding; in their findings the court ruled that neither Captain Howes nor any of his crew were to blame for the collision and were exonerated. After the ***Arranmore*** had touched ground, she lay in such a position that part of her after end became submerged at high water. However, the rise and fall in that region of the world is small in comparison to the UK. Nevertheless, the vessel lay in a beached position on her port side for the next month. Due to the ***Arranmore's*** stranding, the water level left a stained mark half way up the panelled saloon bulkhead, it served as a reminder of her stranding to all who ever entered that compartment, in fact, that watermark stayed with the ship right up to her last days as the *Vindicatrix*. Fortunately, the ship's hull was found to be little damaged and plans were made to refloat the vessel at a later date. When she was once again made seaworthy, the Dutch tug ***Zwarte Zee*** pulled the dismasted sailing vessel back into the water. Because of the lack of local repair facilities - as well as the insurance claim, it was decided to tow the vessel back to the River Clyde.

The ***Zwarte Zee*** was one of two tugs which had recently delivered a floating dry-dock from Europe to Durban. Therefore, as the tug was homeward bound again, negotiations were made for a tow back to the UK. On 3 March 1904, in what at the time was regarded as a tow of record distance, the long haul began; this was to take the ***Arranmore*** back to her native Scotland for a complete refit. The tug was fortunate in having good weather during the tow, so good in fact, that she made an average of six knots for the 7,950 mile haul. During the passage she took on coal bunkers at Dakar before delivering her charge in June 1904, this was after a 54-day passage.

Writing to Sea Breezes in November 1956, J Anderson of Stromness, who appears to have been a visiting shipwright, gave his personal account of *Arranmore's* stranding in 1903.

'I landed at Port Elizabeth in November 1903 from the mail liner ***Briton***; this was the morning after the gale in which the sailing vessel ***Arranmore*** had stranded. There were about 30 ships in the bay, and the wind increased in velocity all day.

I stayed in a small hotel near the sea front, and when I looked out the following morning, the ***County of Pembroke*** of W Thomas's Welsh County Line was ashore almost opposite

From an oil painting by the author

Largiemore

the hotel. Another small wooden barque was still holding on with her masts gone; the ***County of Pembroke*** had swept her sticks out as she passed. From the beach I saw two other wooden barques ashore, they were grinding together whilst the ***Arranmore*** had her spars lying over the port side. Later on I was to meet Walter Ross the mate of the Arranmore, his younger brother who was an ordinary seaman accompanied him. Those two like myself were Orcadians, and from them I was able to hear the full story of the ***Arranmore's*** stranding. Whilst I was talking to them a small foreign barque began to drag her anchor; she then set a topsail and came onto the beach stern first. Her crew were rescued by breeches buoy and immediately afterwards the barque split into two parts. An Italian barque, which had originally been the ***Hospodar*** of Liverpool was also ashore.
Another Italian barque ***Letezia*** was riding on the edge of the breakers, and it appeared as though she was also likely to hit the beach. She held on however, and a few days later I was sent aboard to replace her torn out hawse pipes. She looked a real clipper, and I was interested enough to note she had the name ***Lufra*** carved out on her steering gear box. In her saloon which was lined with birds eye maple, there was a chronometer bearing the inscription of Alexander Hall, Aberdeen. I later learned this ship had sailed under the red ensign in the Tasmanian trade. The ***Letezia*** was a wreck aloft, but due to her composite construction was sound of hull. I also worked aboard the Greenock barque ***Woodburn*** whose windlass had been torn out during the big blow.
Arranmore's stranding had been caused through the fouling of her ground gear by the South Shields Bucknall steamer ***Mashona***; this was in the steamers attempt to escape the bay and reach the open sea. However, the steamer crossed the bows of the ***Arranmore*** carrying her anchors away and sending her ashore. As a result, when the ***Arranmore*** struck the beach her masts went over the port side. The ***Mashona's*** funnel was badly damaged and the figurehead of the ***Arranmore*** was later found on her foredeck.
Ross told me that although the ***Arranmore*** was in ballast, she'd filled her decks before striking the beach. The master's wife and child were aboard but no casualties were recorded. The ***Arranmore*** was eventually re-floated then towed to a Scottish repair yard by the Dutch tug ***Zwarte Zee***; this was one of the two tugs that had brought a floating dry-dock out to Durban.
In 1909 she and her sister ship were sold. The ***Largiemore*** went to the Norwegians and the ***Arranmore*** to the German firm of H Folshe, renamed ***Waltraute*** and registered in Hamburg. The new owners kept the ***Waltraute*** for three years until 1913. But after being dismasted off the Falklands and then on arriving at Montevideo, she was towed back to her home port of Hamburg. It later appeared that repairs would be too costly, and what was left of the ship was sold to the Hamburg Harbour Mission for the price of scrap. Although the ship's sailing days were by that time over, the First World War was

beginning to loom. The German Navy then commandeered the vessel and towed her to Heligoland. The main deck was covered in with additional accommodation and electricity installed; the former Cape Horner was then used as a submarine depot ship.
At the end of the First World War the hulk was captured and taken first to Hamburg, then across the North Sea to Leith. At her new moorings she was once again used to accommodate seamen from the German Navy, although this time in rather different circumstances. These were the men who were awaiting repatriation after the surrender of the German fleet at Scapa Flo. With them there were also a number of merchant seamen. However, 20 months after arriving at her Leith moorings, the ***Waltraute*** dragged her anchors in a big blow: this resulted in the vessel going aground at Inch Keith.
Once again the ship was salved and in 1920 she was handed over to the Shipping Federation. Then on 2 June 1921, the rusting hulk was towed to the West India Dock in London. In 1922 she was given a new lease of life and re-named ***Vindicatrix,*** port of registry London.
The Latin word for Vindicatrix is 'Female Vindicator.'
At the outset of the Second World War the old ship was once again on the move, this time to Sharpness. Under the command of Sydney Angel she left Gravesend on 8 June 1939; the Watkins Towing Co of London undertook the tow. On arrival the hulk was prepared as a training vessel, then for the next 27 years served as a 'first ship' for over 70,000 trainees. Whilst on course the trainees were housed in dormitories ashore, their instruction which included general seamanship, lifeboat and fire drill was carried out on board.

The following extract is taken from: Sharpness A Country Dock. By Wilf Rowles.

In her new role the vessel was under the joint command of Captain FJF Duguid OBE and Captain Sidney Angel. As she locked in on her arrival at Sharpness, the ***Vindi*** as she became affectionately known, was greeted by a number of spectators, amongst them was a local man named Mark Allen. Due to the efforts of this man, welfare and religious instruction was then provided to the young trainees. Mr Allen was a quiet man who felt there was a challenge presented to him, he knew the young lads who'd joined the ship would be away from home, and most of them for the first time. The Flying Angel that was built in 1943, was used by the lads in the evenings after their day's tuition had ceased, and from there Mark gave them the encouragement they needed. Trudging through a heavy fall of snow, feet soaking wet, Mark entered the Flying Angel building with some trepidation and a pile of music sheets under his arm.
A talented musician, Mark was at first asked by the boys if he was a parson; on replying that he'd only come along to play a few songs, he was welcomed into the warmth of the

building. Each evening fair weather or foul, Mark could be seen wending his way towards the Flying Angel to see 'my boys' as he called them. The young lads who came to the school were from all walks of life, yet every one of them was treated by their mentor with the greatest of respect. Each week saw old boys leaving to join their first ship with a new intake arriving. On asking where the *'Vindi'* was lying, those new boys were told to 'see Mark Allen, he'll put you right.' The lads of the *Vindi* thought so much of Mark Allen, that many of their parents sent him letters of appreciation and thanked him for the good work he was doing.

In 1953 he received the BEM in recognition for his services to the boys of the ***Vindicatrix.*** During the 28 years the ship had been at Sharpness, either Mark Allen or the Gospel Hall at Berkeley presented a bible to each of over 70,000 boys when they left. Initially, the money came from Mark's own pocket, though at a later date the YMCA provided the funds.

After the retirement of Captain Angel and Captain Duguid, Captain Poore assumed command of the training ship. However, on 31 December 1966, the 73 year old Merchant Navy Training Ship ***Vindicatrix*** ceased operations at her moorings in Sharpness. Indeed, the old ship had seen much more than her fair share of activity during her long career. At first she'd been a cargo carrier under the British flag, then a German merchant ship, and a Hamburg hostel, before coming a submarine depot and accommodation ship. Unfortunately, it was during her life span in this period as the ***Waltraute,*** that German submarines sank large numbers of British ships. However, the period in which the former ***Arranmore*** will be most favourably remembered, was in the last leg of her life as the Merchant Navy training ship ***Vindicatrix.***

Early in 1967 she was taken by two tugs to John Cashmore's ship-breaking yard at Newport; the National Sea Training School then moved back to Gravesend. After dismantling work on the ***Vindicatrix*** had been in progress for some time, an eleventh hour bid was made to save the vessel from the cutting torch.

This rescue attempt was made by Karl Kortum, who at that particular time was the director of the San Francisco Maritime Museum. Indeed, a man who had himself served under sail. On learning of the proposed fate of the former Cape Horner, from an article written by Charles Wright the first officer of the ***Vindicatrix,*** Mr Kortum sent a series of telegrams to Mr Wright in an attempt to purchase the vessel.

Unfortunately, the reply to Karl Kortum was the dismantling was well in progress with the top deck and saloon having been cut away. The irony of it all was, that if Mr Kortum had opened negotiations a few weeks earlier, the vessel could have been towed to the USA and rebuilt to her 1893 appearance. Mr Kortum was the man responsible for the saving of the ***Wavertree,*** which is now a museum ship at South Street, New York.

Andrina

Although this was a ship of note because of a record she once established, it wasn't exactly a record for sailing, or even being in the water, and neither was it a record her owners wanted. However, it is true testimony to the durability and hard wearing qualities of the iron built ships. The Liverpool registered ***Andrina*** launched in 1886, was designed as a four masted ship but completed as a barque. The Canadian brothers EF&W Roberts were its owners, whilst her builders were Oswald & Mordaunt of Southampton. With a gross tonnage of 2,636, her other dimensions in feet, were 326.6 x 42.9 x 24.9. Besides these measurements she had masts of enormous height, her main truck being some 212 feet above the water.

After the ship had completed her maiden passage to India, a time when George Stailing was her master, the ***Andrina*** was rammed by a steamer whilst homeward bound to Falmouth for orders. The crippled vessel was then towed into Queenstown where lengthy repairs took place. She then continued tramping for the next 10 years. After a normal career of tramping around the globe however, the ***Andrina*** was to enter into the annals of shipping history, this was on a voyage that began at Antwerp in February 1899. Bound for San Francisco with a general cargo, she was expected to arrive there in June or July of 1900. Unfortunately, a mishap near Cape Horn, ensured that the ***Andrina*** would never reach her destination.

After having had a good run as far as the Magellan Straights in mild weather, it would appear that her captain had attempted to pass through the Straights of Le Maire. Others had done it before him, and in good weather it was the accepted thing. However, it was winter in the southern hemisphere and the days were getting shorter. On the night of 10 May 1899 the fog came down, and in the dark under all plain sail, the big windjammer drifted up onto the beach of a little inlet at Policarpo Bay.

After the situation had been assessed at first light, it was discovered that the barque was stuck fast in the sand and mud, furthermore, there was no chance of getting her back into the water without the aid of a tug. Civilisation seemed a long way off. Ships which did traverse Cape Horn normally avoided the Le Maire Straights in the winter months, opting instead for the wider and safer berth of the open sea. The ***Andrina's*** chief officer and four sailors set off in a boat to find help, but probably due to the continuing fog they were lost and were never heard of again. Lookouts were posted at the mast head, and fires were lit on the beach to try and attract the attention of any passing ships, but alas, the grounded crew had to stay marooned on their ship until 7 July 1899 when the ***SS Rio Santa Cruz*** arrived. She was an Argentine Navy supply ship, and on seeing their smoke signals came to the rescue.

The grateful crew were landed in the Beagle Channel, and it was there that they learned there'd been no sign of their missing shipmates. The cargo was discharged from the ***Andrina*** into lighters and barges sent around from Punta Arenas. It was an extremely slow job, as the dischargers could only get near the stranded ship when both the tide and weather permitted. In those years of around 1900, ships of sail were not in demand, and as it was estimated to be too expensive to engage a tug to pull ***Andrina*** back into the water, she was declared a total loss by the insurance company.

Word soon spread amongst the local Indian inhabitants of the derelict ship on the beach, and between them and the scavengers who came around from Punta Arenas in their boats, the ship was soon stripped bare. In that region of the world, timber must have been a commodity in short supply, for not only was all the woodwork taken from the accommodation, the decks were stripped bare as well. Sails, hatch covers, hatch boards, and all the running gear also went, the only removable items the removal experts left, were the heavy iron wire standing rigging, this they probably couldn't un-ship or else had no use for.

In 1901 after the insurance company had paid out, the ship was put up for public auction. There was only one bidder of a few pounds from a Swedish company. The 15 year old iron hulled ship was then left to rot away in one of the world's most desolate places. Then came the test of endurance amidst the vicious Cape Horn weather, and with the ***Andrina*** laying beached on an even keel, she went through all that Cape Stiff could throw at her for the next 17 years. The First World War began, shipping losses were heavy and tonnage was in short supply; by the year 1917 it was so short, that anything at all that could float was considered for service.

Senor Menendez was known throughout the Argentine as the wool king of Patagonia, and as well as controlling a large labour force, he also owned vast tracts of land and farms. Being a keen businessman and entrepreneur, he had undoubtedly been observing the derelict ***Andrina*** for some time, and having already bought the ***Wavertree***, which at that time was his floating wool store in nearby Punta Arenas, he knew full well the true value of the iron built ships. He had the ***Andrina*** surveyed and the results were remarkable, for there was no deterioration whatsoever in her iron hull. Within a short space of time and for £500, the vessel was purchased from its Swedish owner who'd probably forgotten all about her. The task of getting the ship back into the water then began. When the salvage operation started in January 1918, the ***Andrina*** had been on the beach for nearly 18 years. During that time she had settled into the sand and mud by six feet aft and three feet

Andrina *Photo-James Maguire*

forward. It then took over four months of back breaking work by a large labour force of local Indians to dig a huge trench around the ***Andrina.*** During this operation many thousand tons of sand and mud were cleared from around the vessel. On a number of occasions their work was undone when the trench flooded. However, when all was ready in the winter month of June 1918, two Menendez steamers pulled the ***Andrina*** back into the water on a high tide. The tow around to Punta Arenas didn't take long, and it was there that the ***Andrina*** was given a good overhaul and a complete refit.

After the ***Andrina*** had been refurbished and made ready for sea again, the letters Alej were placed in front of the name ***Andrina***; the ship was then renamed ***Alejandrina*** after one of the Menendez daughters. The vessel then loaded 7,000 bales of wool from the floating wool store ***Wavertree,*** and under the command of Captain F Giertsen she sailed north for New York. On this passage Senor Menendez took his wife and three daughters with him, but after having being caught in the doldrums, the pleasure cruise eventually turned out to be an extremely long passage of 92 days. On arrival at New York, the ship caused great excitement in the local press. This was because ships of sail were by then such a rarity, as well as the much publicised fact that she'd been on the beach for 18 years.

Consequently, large crowds who had never seen a sailing ship before flocked down to see the vessel. However, she received even more news coverage when attempting to go to her discharging berth, for it was then discovered that the ship's masts were too tall for her to go under Brooklyn Bridge. To discharge her cargo of wool she therefore had to be diverted.

The ***Alejandrina*** was then given a further dry-docking at New York, and the survey once again found the hull to be in extremely good condition. The gamble of Senor Menendez had been extremely successful in the salvaging of the ***Andrina***; for not only did he possess a first class ship, but the expenses of his acquisition had been doubly paid for with just the one cargo shipment. The ***Alejandrina*** continued to make profits for her owner, her next trip being a grain cargo to London where she arrived in April 1921. However, it was the end of another chapter in the ship's life. According to her owners the Compania Chilena de Navigacion Interoceanica, the ***Alejandrina*** and her sister ship ***Andalucia,*** which Senor Mendez also acquired cheaply, were later anchored in the Punta Arenas Roads.

Here the two ships served a dual purpose; firstly as stationary floating warehouses, and secondly to be used as barges for the short distances between local loading ports. In 1940 both these ships were readied for further sea service, but only used as collier barges when with two tugs in attendance, they carried local cargo to Beunos Aires. In this new extension of life, both ships kept their top hamper and a small maintenance crew. However, neither of those ships were ever sailed again.

The Andrina lay on the beach for eighteen years, and was stripped bare in the process.

Authors Collection

Antiope

Referred to as an iron clipper, the ***Antiope*** was built in 1866 by John Reid & Co at Port Glasgow. A sister ship ***Marpesia*** was also built for the company shortly afterwards. From the same plan, Reid also constructed the ***Benmore*** for another Liverpool company Nicholson & McGill. These three ships measured 242 x 41 x 23 on a gross tonnage of about 1,500 and a deadweight of 2,700. Apparently, this trio were the first ships ever to be fitted with double t'gallant yards.

The ***Antiope's*** first owner was the Liverpool rice miller Joseph Heap who operated the Thames & Mersey Line. Heap eventually had six ships, ***Antiope, Marpesia, Theopane, Cassiope, Parthenope*** and ***Melanope.*** Under his ownership these cargo passenger ships ran from Liverpool to Melbourne, then on the homeward run, they called at Burma and India for the company's rice cargoes. In 1882 however, Joseph Heap sold his six ship fleet to another Liverpool firm of William Gracie and Edwin Beazley. With their new purchase, these men formed the Australian Shipping Company.

The handing over date for ***Antiope*** was 19 May 1882, five weeks later she sailed from London's East India Dock for Sydney. Captain Black was her commander, and on a passage that took 101 days, the ship's complement was 28. The *Antiope* then went to San Francisco before loading a grain cargo for Queenstown and orders. The next voyage in 1884 saw the ***Antiope*** sailing from Liverpool to Melbourne in 84 days, then on her third trip also from Liverpool to Melbourne, she made that passage in 81 days.

The Antiope as built

Photo James Maguire

When Gracie & Beazley bought the *Antiope* in 1882, some weight was taken from her top hamper. The fore and main upper t'gallant yards were removed and she was cut down to a barque rig. She is seen here using her main yard as a derrick for discharging into the coal barge alongside. *Photo Dallas Hogan*

From then on, most of the ***Antiope's*** sailing career was spent in the Pacific where she was regarded as a fast and reliable ship. In fact, she still holds the record for a passage from Eureka in California to Sydney. This was made with a full cargo of timber that included a deck cargo. The record passage was made in 44 days with the distance being 7,130 miles. Despite her speed however, her six iron yards and masts made ***Antiope*** extremely heavy aloft. This induced heavy rolling, and instead of her name being ***Antiope,*** her sailors called her the 'Anti Hope.'

In 1893 the little ship was laid up at Hamburg for 18 months; she then acquired a charter, and under Captain Banks loaded a cargo of general for Melbourne. However, in May 1897 she changed hands once again, this time to Captain George Murray who sailed her himself. In 1904 Murray sold the ***Antiope*** to a Victoria BC company, then two years later Captain Mathieson bought her. The new captain sailed her for the next nine years until 1915, then once again the ***Antiope*** was sold, this time to the Paparoa Coal company of New Zealand for use as a coal hulk. The Otago Rolling Mills were the next owners of the ageing ship, but under Captain Telleck, she was fitted out and loaded at Melbourne for Hobart and Dunedin.

Good sailors were becoming a rarity at the turn of the twentieth century. Therefore, as well as having been cut down to save top weight, her crew could also be reduced to save on wages. Many ship rigged vessels were cut down in this manner for those very purposes. *Photo Dallas Hogan*

On arrival at the New Zealand's south island, the weather was so bad that the tug's line could not be made fast. The consequence was, the fifty year old ship piled up onto the rocks where she stayed for the next three months. Eventually she was hauled off and given much needed repairs and a refit at Port Chalmers. Apparently little damage had been sustained during her 96 days ashore, and no hogging or sagging was found in her hull. Therefore the ***Antiope*** continued trading in the Pacific whilst the war was on. In 1919 at the ripe old age of 53, she loaded a cargo for London. Unfortunately, a dock strike in the British capital diverted the vessel to Rotterdam for discharge, she then sailed to Stockholm to load a cargo of timber for Delagoa Bay.

On arrival at the South African anchorage, and whilst her timber cargo was being discharged into lighters, fire was discovered in the hold in December 1920. Except for a few buckets of sand the ***Antiope*** had no fire fighting facilities. Nevertheless, she remained afloat and the fire was eventually extinguished.

However, the wooden decking, running gear and accommodation had been so badly burned, that the cost of towage and refurbishment to Cape Town was more than the ship was worth. Although the ship's sailing days were over, the iron hull was sound, and the uninsured little ship that had sailed so many miles in her 55 years, was converted into a stationary refrigeration vessel for further use.

Bidston Hill

Built by WH Potter of Liverpool for William Price of the same port, the *Bidston Hill* had a sister named *Primrose Hill.* Both these vessels had been ship rigged on completion but were later reduced to barques. They both met disastrous ends; the *Bidston Hill* off Cape Horn whilst on passage from Hamburg to San Francisco in 1905, and her sister in the Irish Sea where she went ashore off Holyhead in 1900. On both occasions there was heavy loss of life. Contrary to general belief where ships are sunk by Cape Horn's occasional ferocious weather, the *Bidston Hill* met her end by being caught in a windless zone. This was due to an error by Captain Kendall, who in trying to take a short cut, took a chance by passing through the Le Maire Straits in a gentle breeze. What little wind there had been suddenly dropped altogether, and the captain suddenly found he was unable to tack or wear his ship away from the land. Neither was he able to anchor due to there being a no bottom reading on the log line, the ship began drifting in towards the cliff, and the captain who could see his ship was doomed ordered the lifeboats away. In what must have been darkness or with little light left at the time, the captain who had been injured whilst attempting to launch one of the boats, was placed in the starboard boat with his four apprentices and a few sailors. But the masts which came down when the ship hit the cliff face, crushed the other boat in its attempt to get away. There were no survivors from the port boat, and despite a search at daylight on the following morning, neither men nor ship was found. In previous times, the *Bidston Hill* had been around the Horn in all kinds of weather. On one occasion when she took a merciless pounding of wind and wave, she finished up at the notorious Port Stanley shipwrights for repairs. The bill was a staggering £9,500, virtually enough to have a new ship built. The *Primrose Hill* met her doom when her tow-line parted in heavy weather off Holyhead in 1900. In that instance when the ship went ashore, there were fourteen losses of life; Captain Wilson, his wife and the twelve apprentices.

Lawhill

The four masted barque ***Lawhill*** was designed for the jute trade, and coming from the yard of WB Thompson of Dundee was built for Captain Charles Barrie. The ship was launched on 24 August 1892 by Miss Ovenstone, then named by her friend Miss Alexander. ***Lawhill's*** figure head is said by some to be that of Charles Barrie's daughter Barbara, however, other sources claim it is Mary Queen of Scots; the vessel itself was named after a Dundee hillside. The ship was quite unique in a number of ways, one being that although she was afloat for 65 years, a time she came under nine different owners, not once did her name change.

On its completion ***Lawhill*** was 2,942 gross, 2,816 nett, and 4,800 deadweight tons. The four masted steel barque's other measurements were 317.4 x 45 x 25.1 feet; her spike bowsprit was 58 feet in length. Other measurements in feet, were the poop deck 42, foc'sle 33, and Liverpool House 48. The ship spread 38,000 square feet of canvas, with the running and standing rigging weighing in at some 300 tons; the lower yards were 92 feet in length.

Despite having a Liverpool House, the ship was steered from aft where the helmsmen enjoyed the rare luxury of a wheel house, albeit an open one. Forward of the steering position was a chartroom on the fore end of the poop deck. Another luxury afforded the ***Lawhill***'s sailors was, that instead of being berthed under the foc'sle head, or in a deckhouse on the fore deck which was the usual set up, they had their accommodation amidships in the Liverpool House. This structure was in fact part of the ship's hull and not a deck house.

At the time of ***Lawhill's*** building, the new style Liverpool House structure was in keeping with the latest of sailing ship designs. Sailors were much more comfortable in a Liverpool House; a heavily pitching ship would have little or no effect on them when they were off watch, furthermore, they could keep themselves and their clothes dry more easily. The captain, his deck officers and the steward were accommodated aft.

Many other ships with Liverpool Houses were steered from amidships; they used chain and rod steering gear instead of the usual steering gear box or relieving tackles. In the cases of chain and rod gear, the wheel was connected to the after steering box by a series of chains and rods which ran along or underneath the deck. However, despite its many advantages, the big drawback with a Liverpool House was that when the foredeck filled with water, it took a lot longer than normal to find its way back over the side. ***Lawhill*** was Jubilee Rigged, a term meaning that she had no sails above the upper t'gallants. This new style of rig acquired its name because its innovation corresponded with Queen Victoria's Golden Jubilee. The first British vessel ever to be rigged in this 'bald headed or 'stump t'gallant' rig was the ***Duchalburn,*** a vessel which was launched by Barclay Curle of Glasgow in 1887. However, the first vessel ever to use the rig, was the German barque ***Adolph*** of 1877. ***Lawhill*** had an ungainly, clumsy, and to many a sailor an ugly appearance about her with the jubilee rig However, beauty is in the eye of the beholder, and nobody should have been put off by her appearance, because indeed, the ship was noted for her handiness and was an excellent ship to sail.

Gustaf Erikson was one of *Lawhill's* owners, and the last man to operate a sailing fleet,.

Above -Captain Artur Soderlund and his Chief Officer Madri Lindholm.
Below - *Lawhill* Silhouetted against the setting sun in the last of the daylight..

Photos—Victor Penso

As for the masting of the vessel, ***Lawhill*** was square rigged with steel pole masts on the fore, main and mizzen. What made her an oddity however, was the unusual arrangement of the t'gallants being stepped abaft - instead of afore the topmast doublings. Each of these masts from deck to truck were 148.25 feet in height, moreover, the yards were interchangeable. The steel jigger mast being in one piece was fore and aft rigged. The idea of stepping the t'gallants abaft the topmasts wasn't exactly anything new, indeed, a number of American ships had already employed the idea.
In the 1890's, KC Carey who was ***Lawhill's*** first mate under Captain Thomas Cross, later described to the magazine Sea Breezes, that at first the rig was most unusual and confusing. However, once having got the hang of it, he found it far easier to work with.

He wrote: **'As the upper t'gallant yards had both parrels and trusses, they could keep the yards well forward of the mast, as well as the fact that the t'gallant masts were easier to send down.'**

After being completed in September 1892, ***Lawhill*** began her remarkable career. Under the command of Peter Singer she went from her builders at Dundee to Cardiff, then with a full cargo of coal arrived at Colombo after 89 days. In later times she visited Chittagong, and indeed, it was from that very port where she made her longest ever passage for Charles Barrie, one that took 166 days with jute to New York. Her second longest passage was also from Chittagong, a port from where she departed with jute on 18 February 1899, then after being caught in a number of windless zones, arrived off the Isle of Wight after 156 days for orders. On her arrival however, her crew were very sick with beri beri.
That passage eventually ended at Dundee eight days later, in what was to be ***Lawhill's*** last voyage under Charles Barrie's ownership. Jute had always been in demand in the UK, its main use of course, was for the manufacture of sacks and matting. However, the far sighted Indian jute merchants realised they could make and export the sacks themselves. It spelt the beginning of the end for the jute carriers, as well as the mills of Dundee.
Despite the fact the ship had made a lot of money for him, Captain Barrie could see sail was finished and decided to sell his jute ships. ***Lawhill's*** new owners then became the Lawhill Sailing Ship Co, a firm managed by FE Bliss; the vessel was then registered in London.
The following year ***Lawhill*** went under the management of the Anglo American Oil Company. Thomas Cross remained as her captain until the Scot Captain JC Jarvis of Tayport took command in 1902. Captain Jarvis was responsible for the implementation of the labour saving brace winches. Although the conception of the brace winch may have

been a new innovation, the idea itself was not. Many years previously, various ships had used a similar Cunningham system of bracing yards around. Indeed, one of the ships using the idea in a similar manner was the noted tea clipper ***Thermopylae.*** This vessel was not as accomplished as the *Lawhill* in being able to brace her lower and topsail yards around. Nevertheless, she could brace the foreyard with a hand winch situated beneath her boat skids. Whereas steamers were taking much of the trade away from the sailing ships, the Suez Canal had been the last nail in the coffin for them. But to the Anglo American Oil Co it didn't make any difference, and this was because of the route they took around the Cape. For these reasons, the Anglo American acquired a large number of unwanted sailing ships, vessels which were all snapped up for low prices.

Thermopylae

Thermopylae which had been built by Walter Hood of Aberdeen had a brace winch of an earlier style. It operated the lower fore yard only, and was positioned under the boat skids.

From a painting by the author.

For quite some time Captain Jarvis had been running trials with his brace winch. He had in fact, carried out his experiments out on the *Duntrune* before fitting the idea to ***Lawhill.*** The result proved to be an overwhelming success, for instead of having to call on all hands to swing just one of the huge lower yards around, the job could now be accomplished with just a handful of men. The brace winches then meant that two, or even three, of those huge yards could be braced around at the same time - depending on the weather of course.

Life was much easier and safer for the sailors, for instead of being out at the bulwarks, where the possibility of being swept away was always a threat, they could position themselves on the ship's centre line instead . Whereas Captain Jarvis was also responsible for many other inventions on ships, he will be best remembered for his brace winch, indeed, he was known in wide circles as 'Brace Winch Jarvis.' Under the Anglo American ownership, ***Lawhill*** was used for the transportation of case oil from the USA to Far Eastern ports, then on the return passage, she would of course take any cargo available.

In 1904, when Captain Jarvis was making his last trip in ***Lawhill,*** she had some bad luck in hitting Indian Ocean heavy weather. In fact she rolled so heavily, that the mizzen mast came right out of her and went clean over the side. It took with it the main t'gallant mast and much of the main and jigger rigging. The vessel was then jury rigged before making it in to Mossel Bay then later Cape Town to have her cargo re-stowed. Due to the possibility of a long wait to have a new mizzen mast manufactured, she finally left Cape Town for New York without one. In the year 1911, the Anglo American Oil Co began off loading their ships of sail, and ***Lawhill*** was sold to George Windram of Liverpool for the sum of £5,200; her ship's sides were then painted grey. Captain JA Saunders who eventually remained in the ship until 1914 then took command. At that point in time ***Lawhill*** changed hands once more, this time she went to August Trojberg of Mariehamn who paid £8,500 for his acquisition.

During the First World War and especially in 1917, submarines were sinking ships at an alarming rate, the very year that ***Lawhill*** arrived at Brest with a priceless cargo of Australian wheat. After discharge, and because sailing vessels were such easy prey for the U Boats, the big barque remained at Brest until the end of the First World War. There seems little doubt that in being laid up for the remainder of the war contributed to her survival. At the end of the war it was most interesting to note, that of all the captured German deep water sailing ships, a large number of them had Jarvis brace winches fitted; whereas on the equivalent number of British ships - there were hardly any.

In 1919 ***Lawhill*** had Captain Gustaf Erikson as her owner. A Finn from Aland, he was the last person ever to own a sailing fleet. As his flagship ***Lawhill*** was painted white, and under his ownership at the end of WW1 she was a regular visitor to Australia where freights were at an all time high. In 1920 ***Lawhill*** transported 4,800 tons of Australian wheat at 150 shillings a ton, then in 1921 another full load at 120 shillings,. In the following year however, and due to the massive post war ship building programme, the rate had dropped to 40 shillings. In those post war years the ship had acquired the name of 'Lucky Lawhill' with one point of interest occurring in October 1932, whilst she was on passage from Copenhagen to Port Lincoln. In a position just off the Skaw, she collided with the Polish SS ***Nieman*** in poor weather. After the collision ***Lawhill*** lost the stricken vessel in the mist. The steamer eventually sank, but she did manage to get her boats away with the survivors eventually reaching safety. The ***Lawhill*** then went to Gothenburg for repairs to her bow plates.

At the end of her voyage in 1933, a cargo of dressed timber was loaded in the Baltic before the vessel paid a visit to London; then on a later occasion she dry-docked at Birkenhead in 1937. Apart from a trip or two to the Chilean nitrate ports, ***Lawhill*** remained in the Australian grain trade and was often prominent in the 'Last of the Grain Races' an annual event which unfortunately ended at the outbreak of WW2.

Due to the Second World War, Captain Artur Soderlund brought his whole family to the UK for safety reasons, he even brought his much beloved four dogs. When he sailed from Glasgow he had a neutral Finnish flag painted on the ship's side amidships; the ship then went to Mahe before taking guano from Assumption Island to New Zealand. In 1941 the ***Lawhill*** loaded a full cargo of Australian wheat for South Africa. Whilst on passage however, Finland entered the war on the side of Germany. With the full backing of his crew, Captain Soderlund entered South African waters and was escorted into East London by the converted trawler **HMS *Babiana.*** The Union Government placed ***Lawhill*** under the Railways & Harbours Administration then registered the vessel in East London. Captain Soderlund his family and crew were quite content to remain on the ship under the South African flag.

An extract from the Claremont, Cape Town C F P in 1945, states that ***Lawhill*** had a crew of 45 as well as four dogs and a monkey. There was also live stock of pigs and fowl for crew consumption.

Despite the fact that Captain Soderlund had his family aboard, this number of 45 seems quite a generous ship's complement. However, at that particular time there were a number of South African cadets in the crew list. It appeared at the time, that to have 'sail' included on a mate's certificate was a valuable and notable addition, and due to the virtual extinction of sail was extremely difficult to obtain. Under the South African flag the vessel ran to Australia, where as well as grain, large amounts of jarra wood railway sleepers were brought back to Cape Town.

In 1947, the South African Government who had no thoughts of sentiment sold

Lawhill to the Arden Hall Steamship Co for £9,000. Under her new owners the ageing ship made her last two voyages, one to South America and the other to Australia. Later on the four masted barque was sold to an East African businessman from the port of Beira; unfortunately, he could get neither a charter nor a crew. The ship was at that time showing serious signs of neglect, and although an effort was made to keep her in some sort of shape by the shore side people she began to deteriorate. To this end, it would appear that nobody was able to maintain a ship like proper crew of sailors. Later on the once magnificent ***Lawhill*** changed hands yet again, she was then moved to Lourenco Marques. Her days were over. ***Lawhill*** had been in service for 55 years when she ended her commercial career, and that figure in itself was remarkable.

Although at the time she may have looked good from the outside, no doubt her frames had just rusted away, and with all the cement boxes around her keel she would never have passed another survey. What a pity Charles Barrie hadn't had her built of iron instead of mild steel like his beloved *Dundee,* if he had, there is every chance ***Lawhill*** would still be with us today, possibly as a museum ship. Although records don't exist, it is the author's assumption that as a sailing ship, the ***Lawhill*** carried more tonnage around the oceans of the world - as well as sailing more sea miles, than any other merchant ship in the whole history of sail. There is really no set date attributed to the end of ***Lawhill,*** because as she lay idle between 1949 and 1957, bits and pieces went missing off the ship.

The figure head was removed sometime before 1957, apparently to be broken up for firewood by the local natives. Then due to the lack of her being oiled and wet down, the parched decks of ***Lawhill*** shrunk, moreover, the accommodation was stripped by robbers. The late Captain C J Harris of Cape Town, who was once an acquaintance of the author, said that between the years of 1957 and 1958 he was serving on the South African Governments **SS *Dalia.*** At that time, the ***Lawhill*** was slowly being broken up, and ***Dalia*** was engaged in loading the last of ***Lawhill's*** remains into her holds. This cargo of metal was to be transported to Hiroshima for scrap.

With the decks getting squared up, the Blue Peter flying and the holds of the ***Dalia*** full, the ship was being made ready to leave port. Then at the very last moment an excited but unknowing camera bearing tourist came aboard ***Dalia.***

He asked Captain Harris who at the time was on the main deck, for directions to where ***Lawhill*** might be laying, in order for him go aboard and take some photographs of the vessel. The unfortunate but unknowing tourist was taken to ***Dalia's*** still open cargo hatches, and after being shown a load of twisted sheets of scrap metal, was informed that what he was looking at was indeed the ***Lawhill,*** or at least what remained of her. When the coal burning ***SS Dalia*** left with her cargo of scrap metal for Japan she never came back. She was scrapped along with her cargo.

With her wire buntlines in need of slackening off, the *Lawhill* has other pressing problems as the barometer glass rapidly drops. Indeed, it's all hands on deck as the bald headed barque prepares herself for a struggle with the weather. The fore and mizzen upper t'gallants have been furled and the main is next. Meanwhile a sailor out on the end of the bowsprit is taking the upper t'gallant jib-sail in, very soon she'll be under storm canvas.

The SS *Dalia* was scrapped with her cargo of scrap metal.
Photo - Captain Keith Meyer

Captain Artur Soderlund. He commanded *Lawhill* for fourteen years ***Photo - Pim Penso***

Lawhill's **crew during the grain races of the early 1930s. Seated centre is Captain JA Soderlund, a man who should not be confused with Captain Artur Soderlund who later commanded the ship from 1933 until 1947.** James Maguire

Right - With Captain JA Soderlund in command, and a cargo of grain from Port Victoria for Birkenhead, ***Lawhill*** **went aground in the River Mersey on 2 July 1932 .** *James Maguire*

Left - After being dry-docked at Liverpool, it was that found that no damage had been sustained.
James Maguire

Below - Then six months later she was back in Port Victoria.
James Maguire

Above -When Finland entered the war on the side of Germany, Captain Artur Soderlund had the full support of his crew on sailing *Lawhill* into South African waters to surrender.
Cape Archives

HMS *Babiana* was a converted trawler that escorted the *Lawhill* into East London.
Cape Archives

Above - With *Lawhill* sailing into Sydney harbour from Hobart, the King George V class battleship presented a much more daunting sight than the little *Babiana* did.

Sydney Herald

Right - Then with sails furled, her decks tidied up and yards being squared, *Lawhill* has dropped her starboard anchor in Sydney harbour. If needed the port anchor is slung in the cat heads. ***Sydney Herald***

Sunday is a day when a little relaxation can be taken. That's if all maintenance is up to date and the weather is good. ***Victor Penso***

It's an everyday task for sailors to overhaul buntlines, rovings whippings and seizings. Here two of Lawhill's crew are doing just that in ideal working conditions.

Victor Penso

Above - This view from the mizzen shows the jigger staysail has been well sheeted home. With the wind coming from somewhere off the port side.

Lawhill's afterguard at 'smoko.' From left to right - Second Mate Bruno Erickson - Chief Steward Emil Numinen - First Mate Madri Lindholm - Supernumery Pim Penso and Third Mate Phillip Nankin.
Pim Penso was the photographer responsible for this and many of the pictures in this article.

3rd Mate Phillip Nankin.
Victor Penso

2nd Mate Bruno Erickson.
Victor Penso

Chief Officer Madri Lindholm. ***Photo Victor Penso***

Captain Soderlund with his wife, daughter, and two of his four dogs.
Victor Penso

The chippy and a sailor trying to ascertain the huge wingspan of a visiting albatross. Sam, another of the captain's dogs isn't interested. *Victor Penso*

The helmsman steering with the forward of the twin forty eight inch wheels. (The after one is just visible) Whereas *Lawhill's* helmsmen were afforded the luxury of an open wheelhouse, and although it may have been a welcome item in cold or heavy weather, that steel wheelhouse was an absolute sweatbox in the tropics. *Victor Penso*

Above—The builder's plan of the four masted barque *Lawhill.*
Below—*Lawhill* in the Mersey, George Windram of Liverpool bought her in 1911.
Author

Above - With both anchors slung off the cat heads, this picture gives an interesting view of the foc'sle arrangement. *Victor Penso*
Below - Back in Cape Town after an Australian voyage, *Lawhill* is taken in tow by the local tug *TS McEwan.* ***Cape Archives***

Above - Pim Penso took this photograph of somebody's dhobying from *Lawhill's* foreyard.

Victor Penso

Then whilst the ship was making way under a good press of sail, he sat in a bosun's chair hung off the bowsprit to take one of three curious sailors on the foc'sle head.

Victor Penso

Monkbarns

The *Monkbarns* was a well known Liverpool ship that was built by A McMillan of Dumbarton in 1895. Her owners were D Corsar & Sons, a firm that already had a number of ships which was referred to as The Flying Horse Line. Indeed, the figure head of the *Monkbarns* was that of a flying horse, and *Monkbarns* was the last ship the company owned. The full rigged ship had a remarkable and interesting career that lasted for thirty two years, and during her travels she visited most of the world's seaports. A medium sized vessel her dimensions were 267 x 40.1 x 23.6 feet with a gross tonnage of 1,911 and a deadweight of just over 3,000.

One of the ship's more unpleasant memories, was when she was trapped in the ice south of Cape Horn on a 1904 passage towards San Francisco. Caught fast for 63 days in mid-winter, her captain died as a consequence. The trip out took nearly 200 days but she returned to Falmouth with grain after a 110 day homeward run. In 1909 John Hardie of Glasgow bought the ship, then two years later John Stewart gave £4,850 for the vessel.

Most of the deep sea trade was taken up by the steamers, and it was years of hardship for the owners of sail. Although the *Monkbarns* had many an anxious time awaiting a charter, she did manage to keep herself busy on the Pacific coal trade. However, in 1926 when like so many other sailing ships she couldn't pay her way, she was sold for £2,500 to the Spanish firm of Ballener Espanola who were the agents for Brun & van der Lippe of Tonsberg. The *Monkbarns* was then used as a coal hulk at Corbucion in Spain.

Monkbarns caught in a windless zone

Monkbarn's figure head

A deck scene on the *Monkbarns* showing the port side of her main deck. She must have just arrived in port, because the two sailors on the left are busy with the gangway bridle.

Tales From The Half-Deck

This is a selection of short stories told by a number of master mariners who'd served their time in sail. They tell of their days in the half-deck, where hard graft and poor feeding was the norm, and when their wages of between £2 and £10 a year was paid from their own indenture bond. When a young man wanted to be a ship's deck officer, the first requirement for him was to serve a recognised apprenticeship. For this he'd have to pass a medical, need some form of educational background and be subject to an interview with the ship owner.

The indenture fee for the boy's apprenticeship varied from between £20 to £50. This sum of money depended on which company he joined and served two purposes. Firstly the indenture bond paid the young man's wages for the four years of his apprenticeship, as well as most of his food expenditure for his period of 'tuition.' Secondly, since it was probably the boy's parents who'd supplied the money for his bond, it would greatly discourage or reduce the chances of the apprentice from deserting his ship.

In this system of practicalities, the ship owner had ... under his ship's captain, four long years of free labour. It was the norm for ships to carry between four and six apprentices, however, some of them carried as many as twelve. This figure in itself reduced the number of sailors required by the Board of Trade to man the ship, which in turn, saved the ship owner even more money.

It would appear therefore, that the object of an apprenticeship was simply to provide ship owners with cheap labour because on many ships the boy was hardly ever given any tuition and had to learn his trade the hard way with the sailors out on deck. In most cases when there was an absolutely filthy job to be done, such as tarring or bilge cleaning, the apprentices were usually first in line for such unpleasant tasks. Furthermore, it was always the junior or first tripper apprentice who took the brunt.

There were very few captains who insisted on the education of their charges, although when any form of instruction was given, it was graciously accepted by the young officers to be. It was the usual policy for the captain to do all the navigating of his ship himself. Normally he trusted nobody and would bring his own charts and instruments on board, then deny any other person - even the mate - any access to them.

Many second or third mates were unable to navigate, their appointment to the rank was simply for them to keep an eye on the helmsman, the weather and anything unforeseen, but only while the captain was below. As well as doing all the navigating, any change of sail was at all times to be sanctioned by the master.

When in his third or final year of his 'time' - which most apprentices achieved - there was usually some respite for him. By that time he'd be able to perform any of the sailorising jobs on deck, and would probably qualify for the rank of able seaman. Then if he was out of his time and halfway through a voyage, he could then move into the foc'sle on an able seaman's wages... £3 a month! Indeed, there were nearly always vacant positions in the foc'sle, mainly thanks to the many sailors who'd deserted.

Hutton Hall

Condensed from a letter to *Sea Breezes* March 1958 Captain E D Farr.

I began my training on the ***Conway*** in September 1901, then after passing out in July 1903, I signed indentures for my apprenticeship with Charles G Dunn of Liverpool. This was in his ships of sail, where my wages for the first year were £2, followed by £6 for the second, then £10 for the third and fourth. At that particular time the company had no sailing vessels in home ports, and this resulted in me putting in a voyage on the steamer ***Foxton Hall***. The cargo was Welsh coal for the Russian government and the destination Port Arthur. We sailed from Barry in December 1903 and arrived at Port Arthur in February 1904, this was just three days before war broke out between Russia and Japan.
We experienced several bombardments from the Japanese fleet whilst at Port Arthur; this caused the master of the ***Foxton Hall*** to abandon the ship under an agreement reached with the Russian admiral. The agreement was, that the vessel would be delivered back to our captain at Chefoo on completion of the coal discharge. The whole crew were then given passage on the Norwegian coaster ***Frigga*** to Chefoo; where on arrival we were accommodated in the Beach Hotel.
After waiting for a month we were sent to Shanghai as passengers, a place where we spent a fortnight in the Sailor's Home. Soon afterwards we were sent back in the **SS *River Min*** to rejoin our ship at Chefoo - which had since been delivered by the Russians. The ship steamed to Shanghai where an amount of repairs took place, after which, passage was made to Calcutta and a cargo for Hull. On arrival at the Humber I was given leave before joining the full rigger ***Hutton Hall*** in Liverpool's Queens Dock. On the same day I joined we sailed for San Francisco with a general cargo.
The ship left at midnight from the Canning half-tide entrance amongst much confusion. This was caused by some of the sailors joining at the last minute, some of whom were making pier head jumps and all to a man incapable through drink. The only sober people on the ship were the pilot, master, officers, and apprentices. We were towed out to the Tuskar by the famous tug ***Sarah Jolliffe***, on the way we rooted out five stowaways and passed them by line from the poop to the tug's deck. A sack of Liverpool pantiles was thrown on the tug to keep them alive until they reached their native Liverpool. Casting off the towline we made all sail in fairly fine weather. Captain Thurber the master was a fine

seaman from Nova Scotia, and although he paid little interest to the apprentices, we liked and respected him. By some strange mistake at the shipping office, the crew were signed on under the old scale of provisions, which at that particular time was optional. As the ship had only been provisioned with the old scale, this caused considerable friction amongst the crew. However, the matter were remedied on our arrival at San Francisco where provisions to meet the new scale was taken on board; afterwards we lived like fighting cocks, or so we thought. The passage from Liverpool to 'Frisco had taken 115 days, it was without incident, except for a tough month against strong headwinds and gales rounding the Horn. During the latter part of the passage Captain Thurber broke his thigh. The incident occurred when he lent a hand in sweating up a rope, unfortunately it carried away under the strain and this resulted in him falling heavily to the deck. However, Mr Dean the mate made a good job of setting his leg, and after a spell ashore in hospital, the captain rejoined the ship with only a slight limp.

After we'd arrived at 'Frisco half the crew packed their bags and deserted. It must be said however, that this state of affairs in those days was the normal thing at American ports. After discharging and as no freights were offered, we shipped replacements for the deserters, loaded ballast, then sailed for Newcastle NSW on spec. On arrival, Mr Parry the second mate left the ship and went to Sydney to sit his mate's ticket. However, as there were no certificated officers available in Newcastle, our bosun signed as second mate.

We discharged our ballast then went under the tips to load coal for Carrizal Bajo and Caleta Buena on the West Coast of South America. About a week after leaving Newcastle, our 'new second mate' lost the fore lower t'gallant sail. This was during a squall in the morning watch, and so enraged was the captain, that the new second mate was told, "Get to hell forrard into the foc'sle where you belong."

After a consultation with the mate, the captain decided to bring me aft to act as second mate. This was a great surprise as I only had nine month's experience in sail. Moreover, there were other apprentices who were senior to me. However, and on being somewhat taken aback, I agreed and shifted my gear from the half-deck to a cabin aft. On arrival at Carrizal Bajo, the ***Harlech Castle*** which had left port a week before was hard and fast ashore and rapidly breaking up. The ship's crew were ashore in a lodging house awaiting passage back to the UK, and Captain Thurber took the opportunity of signing on their second mate. Much to my relief, I was made third mate and remained so until the end of my apprenticeship.

After discharging part of our cargo, we sailed up the coast to Caleta Beuna where the remainder of the coal was unloaded. No cargoes offered so we took in ballast to await orders. We waited for two months and during which time, an attempt was made to clear the undergrowth from the ship's bottom. For this operation the sailors were kept busy dragging the underwater hull with chains. Then we were directed by the agent to sail to Sydney Heads for further orders. We had another uneventful passage across the Pacific, where on arrival at the Heads, orders awaited us to enter and load a cargo of kerosene shale for Rotterdam. Prior to loading at Sydney, we went into Mort's dry-dock where seven wagon loads of barnacles were removed from the ship's bottom. Kerosene shale is a tricky cargo and liable to shift; therefore we had to rig shifting boards fore and aft in the hold as well as the 'tweens. Every space between the deck beams had to be hand packed during loading, and as third mate I was given the responsibility of ensuring the stevedores carried out this job properly.

On leaving Sydney we had an excellent run to Cape Horn, then after rounding that notorious part of the world, we started congratulating ourselves on the fast passage we were going to make to Rotterdam. Unfortunately, when we arrived north of the line to pass through the North East Trades, we ran into long periods of calm. Eventually, we made the English Channel and ran straight into a dense fog. It turned out to be a real pea souper that lasted all the way up to Dungeness. The ship spent two or three days on short tacks between the English coast and the Varne Bank, but she was continually drifting back and forth.

At last we found a slant through the Straights of Dover, there we found several tugs lying in wait to give us a tow. After the usual hard bargaining between the ship and the tug boat captains had taken place, a tow to Rotterdam at an agreed sum was arranged. Arrival at the Dutch port was made after a 126 day passage. There we heard about the great earthquake that had occurred at San Francisco, this happened while we were running our easting down in the South Pacific. After we'd discharged our cargo of shale into two large Rhine barges, the ship began loading a cargo of pig iron and cement for reconstruction work at San Francisco.

At Rotterdam I only had about three months of my apprenticeship left, therefore, I stood by for the whole time that the ship lay in port; the rest of the apprentices were given home leave, and the remainder of the crew paid off. I left the ship a couple of days before she sailed for San Francisco with her new crew, I arrived in London on the SS ***Batavia* 1V.** So ended my first days in sail, it was an experience which had been tough, but it was one I'd never have exchanged for steam. Captain Thurber also left the ship as well as the firm, this was after a dispute with the ship's husband Captain Kilvert. Captain Thurber then went into steam. Unfortunately, he lost his life soon afterwards when his ship was involved in a collision during fog in the Bristol Channel.

Crofton Hall

By Charles Topp and Adapted from Sea Breezes

As well as the many hardships sailors had to endure in the days of sail, disease was one that often had no remedy. At times when just a single person on board was stricken with one of the many tropical diseases, it quite often developed into a shipboard epidemic. A person familiar with such proceedings was Charles E Topp, an apprentice who served in the ***Crofton Hall.*** Apprentice Topp who came from Blyth in Northumberland had signed his indentures with the Globe Shipping Co of Liverpool; a firm otherwise known as Charles Dunn & Company. On 26 July 1889, he joined the four masted barque ***Crofton Hall*** at Penarth. With Captain T H Lyons in command, there were also three mates, seven apprentices, the bosun, a sail maker, 18 sailors, a cook and the steward. Topp's first voyage was to Rio de Janeiro with coal; later on he received his baptism off Cape Horn before arriving at San Francisco; from there a cargo of grain was loaded for the French port of Le Havre.

After two trips from New York to Calcutta with case oil, the ***Crofton Hall*** sailed in September 1891 for the same destination with a similar cargo. Whilst the ship had been in the American port, Mr Sharp the mate had paid off. Mr Scantlebury was then promoted from second to first mate. On arrival at Calcutta in January 1892 the ship was in for a long stay; the cargo of case oil was discharged then one of linseed loaded for Hull. But the period of stay in Calcutta was a long one of five months, and by which time, the ship had been out from the UK for three years. During Topp's long stay at the Indian City he had been visited by his parents. His father whose ship belonged to Ropners of West Hartlepool was in the same port; he was its master, and as usual his mother accompanied him on the voyage.

One of the rewards a sailor can experience in a life at sea, are the times when he is given a long awaited sight of clear blue water, a cool wind, and crisp clean fresh air in his face. Whilst the ***Crofton Hall*** had been lying in Calcutta, none of these natural luxuries had been available. The clammy heat as well as the mosquitoes in the month of July, ensured that life was extremely uncomfortable for those on board; everybody was therefore anxiously awaiting the day when they would finally leave India behind. On 3 July 1892, the ***Crofton Hall*** finally set sail for Hull, and after such a long voyage, the crew were looking forward to a fair weather passage; with some luck they would arrive home in three to four months. But most unfortunately .... it was not to be! After having dropped the pilot off at the Sandheads, and on the first day out in the crisp fresh air everyone had dreamed of, a violent illness thought to be cholera hit the crew. One of the apprentices Arthur Heslop and the sailmaker were the first to die, and this was just a few hours after being taken ill. Other crew members who started going down were the first and third mates as well as three apprentices which included Charles Topp.

Captain Lyons and the new second mate were unaffected by the outbreak, and those two men did all they could to doctor and nurse those stricken by using chlorodyne and brandy. Two more of the sailors died soon afterwards, and this resulted in Captain Lyons putting the ship back to Calcutta. There were two more deaths before the ship arrived back at the Sandheads, and one of these was Charlie Brown the pigtailed Chinese steward. He was buried shortly before the pilot came on board. On the ship's return to Calcutta on July 13, it was reported that many of the deceased had gone crazy before passing out. Those who were affected and had escaped death were temporarily invalided. Ten of the crew were taken to hospital and the remainder paid off.

Whilst the hospitalised crew members were recovering, there was an inquiry into the whole affair and a great deal of publicity was made about it in the press. It appears without much doubt, that the malady was either cholera or ptomaine poisoning, probably caused through eating bad meat from the harness cask. The meat that was referred to as prairie meat had been shipped in New York on the ship's last visit there. During the passage from New York to India however, the meat had been perfectly good and there were no complaints of any illness. But on arrival at Calcutta some of this meat which had not been consumed, was pickled in brine, replaced in the harness cask, and stowed on the poop. It had been laying there on the deck - in the sun - for the whole of the five months whilst the ship was in Calcutta; none of it had been eaten during the ship's stay.

After the ship had put to sea again, it was only then that the meat used appeared to have been thoroughly rotten. Other suspicions were it may have been the water used to make the brine, or possibly the cask hadn't been airtight. In this case a little of the river water may have entered the harness cask during one of the ship's wash downs. Mr Douglas the second mate firmly believed the problem lay in the linseed cargo, or even in the ship itself. Captain Lyons now had the problem of finding a new crew; the first and third mates both rejoined on recovering from their ordeal, however, the second mate refused to sail in the ship. Captain Lyons then shipped a crew of locals, but they quickly left on hearing of the ship's epidemic: then when another crew was signed they followed suit. When the third crowd joined and discovered the ship's recent history, they made their feelings known and also wanted out. A number of them were locked up for refusing to work. The second mate who'd replaced Mr Douglas died before the ship sailed and yet another of the sailors was hospitalised. However, Captain Lyons eventually sailed for Hull with a new crew at the end of July, unfortunately he had to leave a number of his original sailors in hospital.

The *Crofton Hall* had been built of iron in the Queen's Dock of Liverpool by W H Potter in 1883, she was a four mast barque of 2,127 gross tons: dimensions 301.7 x 39.1 x 23.6 feet. The ship was on passage New York to Dundee when she was driven ashore and wrecked on Sable Island, Nova Scotia in April 1898.

On being discharged from hospital, Apprentice Topp joined the ***Dovenby Hall*** in Calcutta. This was another of the company's vessels, and a ship in which he was to finish his apprenticeship. For the first year he signed on as AB, after which, he was promoted to third mate. Shortly after joining the *Dovenby Hall* and whilst the ship was still in Calcutta, Mr Topp who was at the time an AB saw tragedy once again. One evening as the carpenter was going ashore, he either fell, or else he was pushed off the gangway and disappeared into the water; this was under what was described as rather mysterious circumstances. Some of the sailors accused the mate of being implicated, whereupon the chief officer was arrested. After a trial that lasted several days and with no body being found, the mate was released from custody. However, the captain paid him off. During Topp's service in the ***Dovenby Hall*** he experienced both his longest and shortest sea passages: 183 days from New York to Shanghai, and 29 days from Shanghai to Tacoma, his other passages in the ship were, 120 and 125 days from New York to Calcutta. His last passages in the vessel were from Calcutta, New York, Shanghai, and Tacoma where a grain cargo was loaded for Liverpool. On 10 July 1894 the ***Dovenby Hall*** arrived in the Mersey. Mr Topp had by that time been away on his first trip for four years eleven months and fifteen days.

After obtaining his second mates certificate, Charles Topp went into steam and joined Ropners of West Hartlepool; he served as second mate in the ***Crimdon, Alicia,*** and ***Skidby*** From 1898 until 1902 he was first mate in the ***Conningsby,*** then in 1902 he took command of that ship. Captain Topp continued to serve at sea until 1929.

Dovenby Hall *Author's Collection*

The *Dovenby Hall* was an iron ship of 2,069 tons. Built by Palmers of Newcastle in 1885, her dimensions were 280 x 40 x 24.2 feet. In 1902 she was sold to J Arens of Bremen and renamed *Sylphide.* In 1907 she was sold on to Schramm of Hamburg and renamed *Henriette* Then in 1909 she went to August Bollen also of Hamburg. In 1910 she came under the ownership of Vinnens of Bremerhaven. Later on as a WW1 requisition, she became a possession of the Brazilian Government and re-named *Mearim,* then in 1921 she was sold to Lloyd Brazileiro and renamed to *Almirante Saldanha*, at the age of 43 years she was hulked in 1928.

Cambrian Hills

Condensed from an article told by Capt TP Marshall to Sea Breezes

The last ships to be built for the South Wales Cambrian Line were both full riggers. The first of these two fine vessels was the ***Cambrian King***, which after having been built by Russell's of Port Glasgow, began her career in 1890. The second built by Rodger was the ***Cambrian Hills***. Coming from the same plans, the two vessels differed only in inches, the ***Cambrian Hills*** being 1,760 tons had a length of 260.4 feet: a beam of 38.1 feet: and a depth of 23.1 feet: Her length breadth ratio of almost seven to one enhanced some of her fine passages, and on one particular trip she made it out to Port Pirie from Rotterdam, in 77 days.
During her distinguished career she later came under the ownership of William Thomas who registered the vessel in Liverpool. All her subsequent voyages were either to or from the UK, the Pacific, or Australian ports. Two of her voyages are retold in this chapter, the first by TP Marshall, who like so many others started life as an apprentice. In later years however, he finished at the very top, for after learning the rudiments of sail - and learning the hard way, he was eventually appointed as the Principal Examiner for Masters and Mates.

,,

Young men see visions and old men dreams - and I certainly was a visionary when at the age of 15, I was apprenticed to the Liverpool firm of William Thomas & Co. At that time the company operated between 30 and 40 fine sailing vessels. My father took me to Liverpool to be personally interviewed by Mr Thomas, and I was accepted subject to my passing the Board of Trade eyesight tests - and a bond payment of £50! When both of these conditions had been met, I was passed over to the clerk of the company, who with evident pleasure and amazing celerity, escorted my father and I to a firm of outfitters which he personally recommended.
I couldn’t help the word 'backsheesh' crossing my mind. The outfitter if my memory serves me right was a Mr Duggan, and he sent a thrill of joy through me when he said to my father, “This young man was born to be an admiral.”

However, my father who in being a man of the world was not impressed by this flattery, nor the size of the bill which represented my outfit; Mr Duggan's psychology charmed me, although not my father. My black sea chest - with the letters TPM painted in white - became an immediate treasure and symbol. With indentures signed, outfit secured, and a hurried glance at the River Mersey, we returned to our home at Jesmond on Tyne. Day by day I watched and waited for the postman in expectation of sailing orders. About two weeks passed before I received the long awaited letter, its contents informed me that I was to travel to the East Bute Docks in Cardiff to join the full rigged ship ***Cambrian Hills.***

My father accompanied me on the night train from the north east to Cardiff, and by which time the iron grief had well and truly entered my soul. Our rail transport was generally known as the sailor's night train, and indeed, it was full of seamen travelling to join ships in the Bristol Channel ports. They were in varying degrees of intoxication, and from being jolly to plain fighting mad, some were completely helpless; my enthusiasm for a life at sea was beginning to wane.

In the dim light of the dirty third class carriage where the smell of pipe smoke reeked, I pressed myself as far as I could into the corner to hide the hot tears and tried to sleep. My father was engaged in conversation with a seaman; an obvious cut above the rest who were busy passing the bottle around. He advised my father to buy me a sextant, Nories Tables and some other text books.

Cardiff was reached in the early hours of a cold and wet April morning of 1899, there we found the ***Cambrian Hills*** almost fully loaded under the coal tips. I made my way to the half-deck which was fitted with four bunks, I was the last of the four inhabitants to join, and for this, I had the lower athwartships bunk. To me the half-deck was the epitome of everything foul and made me feel quite sick. On the mate's instructions I changed into my working gear and was soon in conversation with my half-deck shipmates, all of whom were first trippers.

At breakfast time the following morning I was told to report to the Mercantile Marine Office, and I duly arrived to sign on wearing my new brass bound uniform. On the way back along the dock road, a man who was obviously a sailor stopped me and said, "Hello shipmate! I see you're joining the ***Cambrian Hills."***

After I'd agreed he continued by saying, "We're going to be shipmates."

He then told me he'd also just signed on. He also told me he was without money until he went on board, and could I lend him a couple of shillings, a sum he'd repay as soon as we met on the ship. Two shillings was the exact amount of my cash belongings and I willingly handed it over to him, for who could do less for a real sailor in one's own ship? Besides, I was proud to think that a real experienced sailor would speak to such a greenhorn as myself. Nevertheless I wondered how he knew I was from the ***Cambrian***

Hills. It never occurred to me at the time, and at my raw stage of life, that it was my uniform cap badge which advertised the ship to which I belonged. Alas! it later transpired that my sailor hero was not a member of the crew at all, and how I kicked myself afterwards. Indeed, my life as a seaman had begun!
With my new sextant and all the nautical textbooks to accompany it, I sailed away from my home outward bound for San Francisco; I had a feeling of indescribable misery within me, and this was to say nothing of my aching limbs.
At Lundy Island the tug cast off, and under a stiff breeze the ship was heeled over in cheerless weather. Meanwhile as we were washing down the decks, two sailors would draw water from over the side with bucket and line, and they'd continually replenish a large tub on the deck. From that tub we'd bring water to the second mate or the bosun, who in turn would fling it over the deck whilst the sailors scrubbed using their deck brooms back to front. Those buckets which were carried one in each hand, seemed to increase in weight with every journey I made to the tub. How my arms ached in protest, and how the ship's movements were so strange to me; long before we were out of sight of Lundy Island I felt as though I was from another world. Still dazed I tried to drink some tea from the enamel mug of Mr Duggan, I gazed at the sad black mess called tea as its leaves floating on the top, they were so large they looked more like privet hedge leaves. However, time is the healer!
Some time later as my confidence slowly grew, my resolve to stick it out began to assert itself. I admired the towering masts and loved the symmetry of the sails and began to glory in the occasional sea which broke on the deck. How I hated the food though, and I thought then, just as I do now, that it wasn't fit for human consumption. Shanties were a delight, and most fortunately we had a musical crowd of sailors. Everything possible was executed to the tunes which helped so much to lighten the labour. I must have heard every shanty known, and in due course became a leading shanty man myself.
When I went aloft for the first time, the objective was the mizzen top. The second mate directed me to ascend the ratlines on the weather side. He said I would find the climb flatter, and also easier to pass over the futtock shrouds with the ship heeled over. The lower rigging was negotiated without much more than a heart flutter, but the futtock shrouds ran outwards and froze me with fright. I made a number of attempts to conquer this hurdle, and although the spirit was willing the flesh was weak, finally I went through the lubbers hole instead. On the mizzen top I beheld a view which was unsurpassed in beauty and splendour; water and sky meeting all around the ship in a perfect circle! What a wonder - what a revelation. Who could accomplish such a miracle? Certainly no human! Nothing empiric about this scene - the master hand was everywhere in evidence - what a place in which to reflect. This was my first real lesson in the belief of the divine being,

and it brought home as no church or minister could ever do. The lesson was repeated many times before I left the profession which made Great Britain. In fact! the Mercantile Marine is Great Britain.

On attempting to descend via the futtocks, the task seemed even more terrifying. From the poop-deck the watching second mate deduced my dilemma.

"Wait till she rolls to leeward, then the rigging will be easier." He shouted, I gritted my teeth in desperation and almost said aloud, 'How the hell do I get over this top?'

Eventually, good old Mr Evans sent an AB aloft, and with a few encouraging words he showed me the way to do it. When I reached the deck I felt no end of being a sailor. My probationary period was at an end - or so I thought! At any rate I was now in a much better position to take stock, and as a result had a firm belief in myself.

I was now keeping watch and 'lighting the binnacle' a call I was to hear on numerous occasions, until the time eventually arrived when I myself was the senior apprentice; that scornful task could then be allotted to a junior. However, down through the corridors of time, where all the great seamen of our rugged island have passed, simple yet seemingly unimportant incidents like this have moulded or altered many careers. The pity is that some of the bravest and most significant world-reaching events have never been made manifest, and all because of the almost natural penchant of the seaman. Modesty! and in many cases a complete lack of ability to 'put their story over.' In later life and as an examiner of masters and mates, I had abundant proof of this when second mates were given simple essays to write.

Of all the incidents in my life at sea, the celebration of 'burying the dead horse' is one which will always be inscribed in my memory. There's nothing novel about the event for it's carried out on all ships. However, it was my first experience, and those musical sailors who were before the mast made it one to remember. What a model of ingenuity this horse was; canvas, oakum, spun yarn, sacks, seizing wire, bits of wood and daubs of paint all dovetailed into a remarkable pseudo nag on its way out. What fun! What a diversion from the monotony of the cramped life of so called civilisation! What a lot of kids we all became for a while!

We had on board the captain's wife and small son, we also had the owner's brother, and for this we were a little more respectful than usual. Under the patronage of the captain and his wife, seats were provided for our distinguished guests. Many songs were sung and especially those of Bantry Bay. One AB named Evans played the accordion quite well, however, the main event was the hoisting of the dead horse to the main yard arm prior to being slipped overboard. The choir assembled and the dead horse slipped. From now on the sailors were on pay for their work; their advance notes had been worked off.

My first experience of a real gale is also something which is etched in the memory of my very soul. Cape Horn! - Blowing like the very devil. Under lower topsails and a foresail, cold freezing weather and uncomfortably close icebergs.

We'd been trying to beat westward around the Horn, and in the six week process were driven so far to the south, it was no surprise to find that we were surrounded by bergs. I remember Captain Evans saying he estimated one huge flat topped berg to be a hundred miles long. The rigging and the yards, in fact everything, was covered in ice to such an extent, that the shrouds and rigging were many times their normal diameter - almost losing their identity. Indeed, I had so many clothes on that movement was most difficult.

Cape Horn Sailors! No fire wherewith to warm our frozen limbs or dry our sodden clothes. We went to our bunks wet, and if we had the luxury of four hours below we arose in the same wet clothes - still stiff and frozen. On this occasion our bad luck lasted for six weeks in our wet and frozen gear. However, many a Cape Horner has suffered worse, and for much longer periods.

The gale had been blowing for many days and seemed to ever increase. I was in the 8-12 watch and during one night the weather really showed its teeth. How glad I was when I struck the eight bells, then to be relieved and climb into my bunk. It was the same bunk which just a couple of months previous had made me almost wretch, however it was now a virtual paradise and a glorious haven of rest.

It was so cold I knew from past experience that it would take at least an hour for me to thaw out and get my circulation going again. Just after I'd warmed up and was just dozing off, Jack Hulme an apprentice from the port watch came rushing in screaming, "Come on Tommy, all hands on deck."

Growl you may - but go you must. As speedily as possible and it wasn't possible to be speedy - sleepy tired and frightened, I made my way out onto the deck. What a sight! What cold! and how black the night was. Merciful Heaven! what antics the ship was up to. Everything was thick with ice, and the entire decks were filled with frothy seething water. From the mate came the order, "Get forrard and take the foresail in."

Where was forrard on such a night as this? The ship was at times submerged to the top of the bulwarks - the boats were being smashed. The water on the decks was filled with sharp chunks of ice, and they rushed from side to side and from forrard to aft with such impact! Even a small piece of wood dashed against a man could have broken his limbs. The gale was at its worst; it screamed through the rigging like a choir from hell itself, and the shrieking squalls took the descant part. These noises must be heard to be believed or understood, for one cannot understand what one has never experienced. How I arrived forrard I will never know, for as I hung onto the lifeline, my feet were taken from me at regular intervals by the force of the sea. Gasping for air with my arms almost pulled from their sockets I slowly made my way forward. It was only because I hung onto the lifeline

horizontally that I eventually succeeded in making it to the foremast; the sailors were there attempting to clew up the wretched foresail.
Despite the fact I was well wrapped in oilskins and lashed up with rope yarns I was soaked right through. First one sailor then another was knocked down by the incessant greeny black seas. Mr Roberts the first mate was in charge, his voice was drowned out by the crashing of the seas and the high winds. His orders couldn't be heard, and on more than one occasion he was swept off his feet only to be saved by grabbing the lifeline. The lid was really off! I made my way to his side whereupon he recognised me.
"Marshall", he shouted, "Get under the foc'sle head and out of the way, this place is too dangerous for you."
"Yes Sir," I answered.
The sailors were all fine seamen, they knew what was required to clew up the foresail, and despite the fact they couldn't hear the mate's orders they went about their work. The sail was eventually clewed up, and considering the strength of the gale it was made moderately quiet. Then came the order of, "Up aloft and stow" The command was immediately obeyed.
The sailors clambered up the fore weather rigging, first being drenched before getting up and over the sheer pole. Jack Hulme who was a plucky enough lad then said to me, "Our turn Tommy."
Hand in hand to keep contact, we started up the weather rigging and made our way aloft. It was as though the entire power of all the worlds hurricanes were combined to pin us to the rigging; our progress in ascent was slow. The gale pressed me so hard to the ratlines my tongue was sticking out of my mouth, and the hailstones hurt so much they inflicted neck and facial injuries.
We reached the fore top though not the yard itself, then hung onto the chain sling with our arms and not our hands; our fingers were frozen and quite useless in the situation. The noise of the sail flapping, the wind screaming and the crashing of the seas defies description. Time after time the sailors had half or more of the sail on the yard in an attempt to secure it. They would hold onto it with their stomachs, only to find that time and again a fierce squall had ripped it from them; then the procedure would have to start all over again.
The sailors were in terrible danger of being blown off the yard, the sail itself was frozen like concrete, they then had to beat on it to loosen the ice to get sufficient grip. It must have been 3 am when we went aloft to stow, and at 6 am we were still there. With the sail now split it lashed fiercely and the men were in danger of serious injury. The sailors were in a bad way. Some men had finger nails completely torn out in trying to grip the frozen sail, and all had facial injuries where the flapping sail had struck them. After it had been

secured, we were so frozen the next hazard for us was to descend to the deck. When the men did arrive on the deck, they all looked as though they'd been in a fierce battle, and indeed they had!
It was later discovered that a number of the sailors had frostbite, some had nasty cuts, while the rest had sprains or bruises. Indeed, it was a number of weeks before the last of them recovered from his injuries. If I were to live to be a hundred years of age, I would always be proud to have known and worked with such men. We duly arrived at our destination where after two of the apprentices had skinned out, we discharged our cargo of coal, then loaded one of grain for Cape Town.
By this time the Boer War was in progress, and our delivery of grain was for the troops. Rounding the Horn once more, the good ship ***Cambrian Hills*** arrived at Table Bay. We anchored amidst a virtual forest of sailing ships' masts, and indeed, there must have been in the region of 50 vessels there.
Taking the Old Man ashore each day was a job for the apprentices, but because there were only two of us left, this job was occasionally reinforced by a couple of ABs. As one apprentice manned the tiller in taking the master ashore, it was the normal routine for the other one to stay on the ship and polish the bright work. On one particular day when it was my turn to stay aboard, one of the mates said to me, " Marshall get your brass and rags, then polish the bright work on the cabin skylight."
Soon afterwards with the ship rolling lazily at anchor and everything quiet, the mate disappeared below; in all probability to have an afternoon siesta.
The skylight was open, and I could look down and see the lovely mahogany furniture as well as the spotless white paint work in the captain's cabin.
In my endeavors to polish the brass rods which covered the skylight, I used old robands well covered with brick dust to reach into the crevices. However, the devil is a wily person, and it was he who put a thought into my head by remembering a previous task.
It so happened that a few days previously, I'd been engaged in helping the steward. The task had been stowing some boxes of currants and raisins in a little locker over the captain's settee. I could now see this little locker from my position of employment. Furthermore, the steward had left its door open! The outcome of it all was my sliding through the skylight, filling my pockets with currants and raisins, then returning at speed from whence I'd started. I continued with the brass work while regaling myself from time to time with a handful of the luscious fruit until it was all finished.
Knock off time came, and with it the arrival of the captain's boat from ashore. After tea time the mate came into the half-deck and told me the captain wanted to see me. Guiltily I entered his cabin, then with a show of great ostentatious bravery, I said in a voice not altogether devoid of a quiver, "Send for me Sir?" To which the captain replied, "Yes

Marshall I did, have you been in my saloon today?"
Silence!
"No Sir."
"Oh!" went on the captain.
"Been working on the poop today Marshall?"
"Yes Sir."
"Cleaning the brass work Marshall?"
"Yes Sir."
The captain stood up and advanced towards me, took me by the wrist and extended my hand to the currant locker. It was then that I saw on the immaculate paint work, the imprint of a hand made by brick dust. The captain placed my quivering hand over the imprint which fitted like a glove. The end of this little tale is forever imprinted in my mind - just as the scars of the rope's end were imprinted on my buttocks - my corporal punishment was administered personally by Captain Evans!
However, an even more painful episode was forthcoming; it was whilst we were in the Atlantic and where I was suffering from severe toothache. At long last and unable to bear the pain any longer, I went to the Old Man and implored him to do something about it. He examined my mouth, and in his probing discovered a hollowed out back tooth. On trying one tincture after another, he then arrived with a sinister looking pair of forceps. Then after a further scrutiny of the hollowed tooth, he exclaimed in his strong Welsh accent. "There's nothing to get hold of man."
He then suggested to leave well alone. Later on and still in agony, a conference was called between the captain, his wife, and myself; at length it was decided that the offending nerve must be burned out. It was the only way! One of Mrs Evans's steel knitting needles was requisitioned for the operation, and this was held over a burning candle until it was white hot.
"Open your mouth wide Marshall and keep quite still."
The captain assured me it would all be over in a second. With a quick jab he aimed at the dreadful cavity. He missed! Instead he hit my tongue with the dreadful red hot atrocity. The result was the toothache vanished. Which proves that the end doesn't always justify the means.
During my tenure on the ship after joining at Cardiff, I went to Cape Town, Newcastle NSW, back to 'Frisco and loaded for Hull. This ended a two year voyage. On rejoining the ***Cambrian Hills,*** we loaded on the Tyne for 'Frisco then straight home to Limerick. On our arrival we sailed right up the River Shannon tack on tack to the lightening ground without the aid of a tug. My third voyage was from Cardiff to Esquimalt with naval stores, then to the Frazer River to load tinned salmon for London. This completed my four year

apprenticeship. I packed my gear away - complete with the £8 sextant which I'd never been allowed to use. (Even the second mate was forbidden to use his.) I had studied hard and felt ready to sit my second mates ticket, however I did go to school for a while to familiarise myself with what candidates refer to as examiner's 'pet questions.'
My apprentice shipmates in the ***Cambrian Hills*** were Harry le Clere and Percy Topham - both of whom deserted in 'Frisco - Jack Hulme who deserted on the second voyage, and Jimmy Nicholson who swallowed the anchor after one trip. The following two, Elliot who was a Conway boy and Humphreys, were still serving on the ship when I left her in 1903.

THE LAST VOYAGE OF CAMBRIAN HILLS

This story was written to Sea Breezes by GCA Archer. He also joined the ship as an apprentice ... a year after the author of the last story had left her.

,,,,,,,,,,,,,,,,,,,,,,,,,,,,

The ***Cambrian Hills*** was an 1882 product of A Rodger & Co of Port Glasgow, she was a three masted full rigged ship of 1,700 gross and 1,632 nett tons. With a length of 261 feet and a beam of 38 feet, she could carry 3,500 tons; the vessel was owned by William Thomas and registered at Liverpool. The ship had pleasing lines in carrying double t'gallants on the fore and main, with just single t'gallant on the mizzen, and all were nicely proportioned. The three courses clewed up to the quarters, and when all her canvas had a harbour stow she had a distinctive appearance. Indeed, the ***Cambrian Hills*** looked a really smart ship.
The vessel was at the time under the command of Captain W Williams, and with him he had Mr JH Owen as mate, Mr EL Phillips as second mate, and the senior apprentice Mr EH Humphreys as third mate. Then there was the carpenter, cook, steward, 14 ABs, and four apprentices making a full complement of 25 hands. The voyage began at Newport with a full cargo of coal, and she left on the evening tide on 16 May 1904 bound for Caleta Coloso. I was a first trip apprentice, and having joined a few days earlier had arrived with new kit and a few hopeful illusions. However, the latter was soon to be rudely shattered.... in a very short space of time!
The half-deck with its four bunks was situated under the poop-deck, forward on the starboard side; the occupants were Hutchinson a third tripper, Roberts a second tripper, Malcolm and myself; we were the green horns. As Mr Humphreys the senior apprentice was acting as third mate he dined in the saloon. The passage out was made in 85 days, and this was considered as being a good run in mid winter. There was only one event of note

that I can remember, and this occurred on the outward passage some days after rounding 'Cape Stiff.'
We were bowling along at 10 knots with a strong wind on the port quarter, the ship was making a good northing, and had already arrived in warmer climes. The lookout was relieved at 5 am to make himself some coffee. However, when he returned to the foc'sle head his relief was absent. He immediately raised the alarm, and after a hasty search of the ship there was no sign of him. The second mate who was on watch called the master, he in turn decided nothing in the circumstances could be done for any rescue attempt; this was due to the time which had elapsed since the man's disappearance, the speed of the ship, and the fact that it was dark. The missing AB was a middle aged Briton of secluded nature; he held himself aloof from any sing songs or other simple amusements such as we had. The general opinion was he'd deliberately gone overboard in a fit of depression; this was when all except the second mate and helmsman were at coffee; I was on watch at the time.
However, this sad event had an impression on all of us, for whatever his temperament he was still one of us.
Arriving at Caleto Coloso we dropped anchor at 1.40 pm on 9 August 1904; there were three other vessels already at their moorings, the German ***Reinbeck,*** AD Bordes ***Chile,*** and the Italian ***Principessa Napola.*** After having discharged part of the cargo by basket, we left on Saturday 17 September 1904 for Iquique. There was enough of the cargo left in the ship as stiffening, therefore, it did not necessitate the sending down of the royal yards. The day before we left a kedge anchor was run out; then on sailing day, we were able to heave the ship around after the bower anchor had been raised, we then stood off in the breeze. At 9 pm in the dark, on Monday September 19, we dropped anchor at Iquique. The next morning was a real eye-opener for me, for here there were dozens of ships all laid in tiers and in all sorts of trim. Amongst the tiered vessels were two of William Thomas's ships, the four masted barques ***Crocodile*** and the ***Kate Thomas***. To our dismay we were told that the remainder of the coal had to be discharged in bags, this was not fun, as the ones who had to do it were well aware.
By the Tuesday we'd moved into the tier, and in due course took on nitrate stiffening. We finished our discharging, and by Friday November 22 our loading was complete. There had been many delays at Iquique, and this was mainly due to the lack of lighters as well as the days when no cargo was available. The loading had been stretched out over two months, and this was apparently the normal thing. On the evening of November 26, we hoisted our Southern Cross lights, cheered the ships in port, then went aft for our grog. We then turned in full of anticipation for the homeward passage. On Sunday November 26, we sailed for Le Havre, with a full cargo of nitrates for the government of France.

After we'd rounded the Horn and were washing down the decks in the Atlantic, a knife fight between two ABs occurred. The gladiators were Julius, a big heavily built Finn with a huge smile, and a man who was quite a power when hauling on a rope. He was a general favourite with all except for his watch mate Scottie; a small wiry man of uncertain temperament. These two had been at loggerheads for quite some time, and the culmination of it all came on this particular morning. After a heated argument and a tussle between the two, and before anyone could intervene, Scottie drew his knife and aimed a blow at the abdomen of Julius. Fortunately, the big Finn spun around resulting in the blade entering his buttock making a deep wound. Scottie was overpowered; the wounded sailor who was bleeding profusely was bandaged up. Julius was then laid up, his mattress and blankets were brought to the upper sail locker, and there he remained until he was able to resume his duties. Previous to this incident, Scottie had been noted grinding his knife to a fine point; this may, or may not have been for the premeditated purpose of a duel with Julius. Nevertheless, that was generally believed to be the case.

In the performance of their duties sailors have to carry knives. But there has never been a reason for those knives to be sharpened to a point. Indeed, there is no task on any ship that requires a point on any sailor's knife. Therefore, it was common practice on ships for the first mate to occasionally inspect sailors' knives. If any are found sharpened to a point he would promptly break the end off.

Scottie was of much smaller stature and of a physical disadvantage to Julius. What the outcome of this affair was after our arrival home I cannot say, because other events which supervened put this affair completely in the background as it were. I went to another ship and never met any of my shipmates again to discuss the incident.

Drawing into the northern latitudes in late February 1905, some spells of bad weather were experienced; in one stiff blow when on the port tack we lost our longboat. By early March we were nearing the English Channel, and everybody was looking forward to the ship's arrival at Le Havre. The heavy weather continued, and the cloud which obscured the sun made Captain Williams an anxious man.

On the night of Wednesday March 8, when 101 days out, we were hove to under storm canvas - three lower topsails, a foresail, and a fore topmast staysail; at the time, there was a SW gale blowing with thick rainy weather. At 4 am on the 9th the foresail was furled, then during the 4 - 8 watch, the wind veered to WNW. Still blowing hard, this gave better visibility except for when the hail storms descended upon us.

At 8 am when in 50-42N and 7-17W, the master decided to square away and run for his projected course; all hands were kept on deck. The helm was put up, and the mizzen yards checked in a little, but quite strangely, the ship refused to pay off. The foresail was then loosened with still no reply, it was at this stage that the master decided to wait awhile. The

mizzen yards were braced up again, the wheel relieved, and the second mate's watch went below. My watch mate Hutchinson and I had a breakfast of coffee and biscuits, and as it was 'vittles day' we had nothing else and turned in.
When nicely under the blankets another squall came down; however after it had passed over the increased list seemed to remain although it was hard to define; owing to the ship's labouring, she certainly wasn't behaving normally. Soon after I heard a lot of commotion in the upper sail locker which adjoined the half-deck; a hatchway situated there gave access to the 'tween deck. The noise of feet clambering down the iron ladder was followed a minute later, by the same feet making a most hurried return. A few moments later a shrill whistle was followed by the cry, " All hands on deck ... take to the boats ... abandon ship!"
Hutchinson and I were dumbfounded, startled or not we quickly tumbled out of our nice warm bunks and especially on hearing the word 'boats.' We found in our hurried dressing that the list was something of a hindrance. Then when we arrived on deck, we discovered that the lee rail was tending to become awash with the lee scuppers well flooded through the freeing ports. It later transpired that Captain Williams had gone into the hold, only to find with horror and amazement, about five feet of water in the lee bilge; hence the hurried steps we'd heard.
The mate's watch attempted to get the lifeboat away from atop the forward deck house on the starboard side; in doing so they used the fore t'gallant halyards. This proved too much for their powers, and with the rolling of the ship the boat smashed up against the deckhouse. During this operation a young Negro AB named West, suffered severe facial injuries. The only boats now remaining were the two on the skids and the gig. By this time the boat falls had been cleared from their sea stow and the lifeboat made ready for hoisting; the port watch then came from forrard to assist. Captain Williams took charge of the boat's launch, whilst the first and second mates and two ABs busied themselves with the gig on the other side which wasn't too much bother.
The lee rail was now awash, and the water was right up to the hatches. The ship was clearly doomed! The launching of the lifeboat proved to be a heavy task, the overriding factor was - that no risks whatsoever could be taken. Indeed, getting the davits and boat swung out against the increasing list was only achieved by a group of desperate men. In being lowered, the boats had to be eased from off the ship's side with the oars and capstan bars, and four ABs went into the boat for this purpose. The steward then hurriedly threw tinned corned beef and biscuits wrapped in the cabin table cloth into the bottom of the boat, this was as the boat was being lowered on its falls.
Considerable excitement and consternation reigned during this hazardous operation. Here was our last seaworthy boat in the process of being launched, down the weather side of a

heavily listing rolling ship.... and, into a big sea! By skillful management and much shouting to boot, the boat was successfully floated and the falls cast off, she was then maneouvered around to the stern. No risk was taken to bring the boat alongside again; the end of the lee main brace was passed over to the boat's crew and they hung her off over the lee quarter. With four men in the gig and four in the lifeboat, the remaining 16 of us had to go hand over hand along the lee brace to make the lifeboat, each of us receiving a good ducking.

I remember well casting off my seaboots for the passage down the rope, then the rise and fall of the sea as it jerked the rope from my hand. I found myself floundering and scared. However, the boat surged towards me and I was hooked and pulled aboard to safety though thoroughly cold and wet. One by one the remaining crew members came along the rope with varying fortunes, until the last man Captain Williams came aboard as cold and as wet as the rest of us. The gig then came towards us as they had no provisions, so we threw them some of our corned beef and biscuits, they then made their way to leeward. No time was lost; we cast off and ran carefully some way down the lee side of the heavily listing ship.

The captain then headed the boat clear, I can't remember whether or not we streamed a sea anchor; the time was now about 10 am. Nobody had saved anything except himself; all we had was what we stood up in, and those who'd received a good soaking shivered in the cold. The boat was leaking, and to bale her out two tins of corned beef were opened and their contents passed around; the hard tack biscuits had become wet, although at this time there was no need for them. About 20 minutes after we'd cast off, the ***Cambrian Hills*** heeled over, and slowly went down broadside on. As the sea lifted us on each swell we watched this calamitous spectacle. The lower yards dipped first, and so on in turn until they reached the lower topsail yards which were set and soon to disappear. Then there was an explosion, and debris flew into the air and dropped. It was the end of the ***Cambrian Hills.*** A sad sight if one thinks back to just a couple of hours previously when the ship was sailing along quite normally. Now our home had vanished before our eyes, and even the strongest nerved amongst us must have felt we wouldn't last long if help didn't come quickly. The poor Negro Mr West moaned in agony at his injuries in what was hard to express. Cold and wet, a bitter wind with hail, squalls and heavy seas pounding our overcrowded deeply laden boat. Some little time elapsed before someone cried out, "A ship!"

Those in the gig must also have sighted her, they'd hoisted a flag on an oar then ran off to leeward towards the approaching vessel. The sombre silence changed and there was a cheer giving vent to our feelings. As she made slow headway into the heavy seas, it took about an hour for her to reach us, it was the Elders and Fyffe steamer ***Oracabessa***. Luckily

and on a clear horizon, she'd spotted the last moments of the ***Cambrian Hills*** as it sank, she then made her way towards us. The gig's crew were the first to be picked up, then after the steamer had placed herself to windward of us we went alongside her. The rescuer's ropes were cast towards us, and willing hands secured our boat alongside, then when we climbed their pilot and Jacob's Ladders, they helped us aboard. Some of our chaps who were suffering cramp had to be hauled aboard whilst the rest of us struggled up the ladders. As each of us climbed over the rail we were given a stiff tot of brandy; mine gave me quite a kick, however it didn't stop me from shivering. When we were all aboard the boats were cast adrift and the Banana Boat steamed towards Queenstown to land us.
Aboard the ***Oracabessa*** every kindness was shown and the crew even gave up their bunks for us. Most of us turned in while our clothes were being dried in the stokehold. It took me a long time to get rid of the shivers, even when I was in a nice warm bunk in an equally warm foc'sle. Such needs of clothing as we had were met from the ship's slop chest and some members of the crew. I was given a pair of boots by someone and these were all I needed. At about 11 pm on the same day, the ***Oracabessa*** made the entrance of Queenstown harbour; then somewhere off Roche point we were transferred to the sailing pilot cutter ***Maid of Erin***. When we were all aboard we gave three cheers to our rescuers, the steamer then resumed on her voyage, which was from Barry to Port Lunon and Costa Rica for bananas.
The pilot cutter tacked her way up the harbour, and during which time, I was below relishing the hot coffee on offer, it even had the luxury of milk in it, as well as bloaters, bread and best butter. Those who'd been on the old ration scale of provisions, will be able to appreciate our great gusto at this sample of shore grub. The pilots just like the crew from the banana boat did all they could by treating us very well. In the early hours of Friday morning we were all landed to be taken to the Sailor's Home. We must have been a queer looking lot in all our different rigs, as we disembarked from the pilot boat at Queenstown.
At the Sailor's Home they were awaiting our arrival, and we were given beds without any fuss. Captain Williams and Mr Owen went to Liverpool soon after, and on the following day the rest of us left for Cork on the 4 pm train. There we boarded the steamer ***Kenmare,*** and after a miserable passage arrived at Liverpool on the Sunday afternoon. We were met and taken to the Sailor's Home in Canning Place, where previous arrangements had also been made to receive us. A day or so later I went home.
At Solva and Newgate in St. Brides Bay, Pembrokeshire, wreckage from the ***Cambrian Hills*** was later washed ashore. Amongst these items was our lifeboat, several spars, and part of the chartroom with the bell bearing the name ***Cambrian Hills*** still attached. At the Board of Trade inquiry regarding the cause of the foundering, the master and crew were

absolved from all blame. The ***Cambrian Hills*** was deemed to have been entirely seaworthy and properly found when she'd left Iquique. The most likely cause of her loss was, that she'd sprung a leak due to the heavy weather.

Cambrian Hills Crew Photograph

Lifelines and Safety Nets

The setting up of lifelines and safety nets on sailing vessels was an almost everyday occurrence, and all due to the fact, that under optimum sailing conditions, those ships were purposefully sailed heeled over. Indeed, the captain of a sailing ship was quite happy to be sailing along heeled over at ten or fifteen degrees. It usually meant that a prevailing wind was coming from the quarter, the sails braced over to the required angle, and in being full of wind was reeling off the knots. Consequently, everything on the ship would be heeled over accordingly; the crew who may be having their meal would have wet burlap spread across the mess-room table to stop their plates sliding off. Their pint pot mugs used for coffee or tea would be only half filled … otherwise the contents would roll out of the mug.

In good weather when a ship had her yards pointing to starboard, and the port or lee side was under water, any work which had to be undertaken by the sailors on the lee side, meant that lifelines and nets had to be rigged. If for example a big sea suddenly came over the lee bulwarks, the men working there would have something to grasp and hang on to. On the other hand, if there were no lines rigged they may well be washed overboard or smashed up against the bulwarks or other. The general practice for sailors on seeing a big sea rushing down the deck towards them, was to leap up and grab the lifeline with both arms and legs also wrapped around it … then wait until the roar of water had subsided. Some of them didn't make it, because another deluge may well have followed on the next head pitch. There have been countless occasions of men being washed overboard and lost after an invading sea has come aboard, and also many who have been badly injured by being thrown from one side of the deck to the other.

In heavy weather when pitching and rolling heavily, life lines and nets were left rigged on both sides night and day. Under inclement weather conditions, the ship may not even be heeled over, but taking seas on both sides whilst rolling heavily. However, in bad weather or good, the decks still had to be manned for both bracing the yards and going aloft. Before the days of compulsory load lines which were implemented by Samuel Plimsoll, a ship's captain could carry as much as the space in his hold would allow. The result of this was, that many ships left port overloaded with reduced freeboards.

If the lifeline was missed, the safety net might save you from going over .... If you were lucky!

Even in good weather like this, a ship that was heeled over still shipped plenty of water.

This in turn, caused the decks to become awash even in good weather. Then when the weather did deteriorate, it can only be imagined the fury and carnage on deck as seas came up and over the bulwark tops. Some of the later and larger ships which had Liverpool Houses carried flying bridges. Also referred to as catwalks, they were not dissimilar to those of the modern day oil tankers. They usually led from the poop deck to amidships and could easily be erected and dismantled.

Flying bridges were seldom set up on the foredeck of sailing vessels, because in being a temporary rig they faced the onslaught of head seas and were often washed away. Indeed, ships that had a Liverpool House often had their foredecks filled to the gunwhale tops and lifelines were most essential on the foredeck, a foredeck which was in fact a well deck. Well deck ships had their own additional dangers of filling up after taking a deluge over the foc'sle. It took a long time for the water to go through the freeing ports and back over the side. In such cases the sailors had to hang on to the lifelines for long periods, and many were lost this way. And neither does size count for safety. The Liverpool registered ship *Liverpool* which was at the time the world's largest merchant sailing ship, once had her well deck filled and lost the whole watch of seamen over the side, including the supervising mate.

A big 'green 'un' coming aboard

In this dramatic deck scene where a lifeline is being rigged, the sailor working under the boat skids has beaten the incoming sea by leaping up and hanging onto the sheer pole. On the far right the safety nets are visible.

One old adage amongst sailors has always been, that it is much safer to be working up aloft than down on the deck.

AETHELBERT

This condensed passage from Sea Breezes was written by Captain FJ Thompson OBE. Here he describes his 1895 experiences on the *Aethelbert,* a ship that left Montrose on 15 April 1896 on passage to Fremantle. At that particular time, the *Aethelbert* was owned by Gracie Beazley of Liverpool

Although considerable improvements had been made in the previous decade regarding the Board of Trade provision of food, and especially with the addition of lime juice, it was still hard going. There were no refrigerators or ice boxes in most ships, consequently fresh meat and vegetables were only available for three or four days after sailing. Salt beef and pork were carried in harness casks; these were brass bound oaken barrels in which the meat was salted down. 'Harriet Lane' (tinned meat) was served on Sundays and Thursdays; potatoes after the first month were unknown except for an occasional supply of the dried variety. Bread was also a scarce commodity, and one 'rootie' - a small loaf - was supplied on Sundays, Tuesdays, and Thursdays, this was sufficient for one meal. The main standby was hard tack which were Liverpool pantiles; these were large biscuits with 52 holes in each of them, the main component of which was bran. They were so hard they could be thrown at the bulkhead across the half-deck without breaking, and it was only a good set of teeth that could tackle them. Their greatest trouble was they were always full of weevils and frequently became mouldy. One pound of butter (doubtful?) and one of jam was served weekly to each man, but no mustard, pickles, pepper, or milk was provided; the apprentices received the same allowance as the sailors.
The apprentices usually started out from home by bringing with them a tuck box for the voyage; this would often consist of jam, sardines, tinned salmon, cocoa, biscuits, as well as a few other little luxuries that were never provided on ships. Ship fare was hard on growing apprentice boys, and many of those on their first or second voyage would often 'pawn' their clothing with the sailors for marmalade or butter. One apprentice I knew of would sit down and eat his pound of marmalade 'neat' as soon as it was issued. He'd then do without for the rest of the week, unless of course he was able to swap a shirt or a plug of tobacco with one of the sailors for his allowance. Tobacco was obtained from the captain's slop chest at three shillings a pound, this was after the master had taken it out of the bond at 10 pence a pound. (A 360% profit for the captain)
The rest of the slop chest realised 100% profit for the captain. sailors frequently went to sea ill clad, they then had to mortgage their pay to obtain clothing from the slop chest.

Many sailors deserted in foreign ports, therefore they couldn't have collected their wages. Although the victualling was of inferior quality, the cooking was worse and brought out the old adage, 'God sends the food, and the devil sends the cooks'.
Memories are short however, and once ashore enjoying fresh fruit and vegetables, the previous hard living on a ship at sea is soon forgotten. We received little sympathy on land when speaking of hungry ships, for as youths we were sun and wind tanned, broadened with constant hard work on deck and aloft, and in general we looked quite healthy.
Our voyage from Montrose turned out to be an adventurous one. The ship being in fine trim made some excellent runs as well as taking part in ocean races with other ships; we overhauled and passed most of them including the noted ***Derwent*** of London.
The usual ceremony took place in the 'crossing of the line' with King Neptune and his satellites coming aboard. This was much to the discomfiture of those making their first voyage who were shaved and ducked.
Running our easting down, the ship had been bowling along at 12 knots, the wind was abaft the port beam was freshening. In the second dog watch we were ordered to shorten sail and took the fore and main t'gallants in. Working in the dark, Highton, another apprentice who was the son of a parson, was working with an AB furling the main t'gallant sail; they were out on the weather yard arm when Highton lost his grip and fell backwards off the foot-rope. Due to the press of sail, the ship was heeled over at 25 degrees to starboard, and the cry of 'Man Overboard' was made. All hands rushed to the main deck and the mate threw a lifebuoy over the side; however, and in the darkness, the chances of him being picked up were hopeless.
Suddenly, and to everyone's surprise and relief, the voice of Highton was heard halfway between the masts.
"I'm all right sir" to which the mate replied in a strained but much relieved voice.
"Come down then, damn it."
Highton later told us he struck the fore t'gallant brace as he fell backwards; this brace ran from the fore t'gallant yard arm to the main topmast head. The impact threw him onto the main topmast stay which he grasped with both hands, then climbed up the stay and down the ratlines to the main deck: his only injury was a slight scratch under his chin. On reporting to the captain who was on the poop deck, he received the comforting remark, "Well my boy, you were evidently not born to be drowned".
After a passage of 93 days we dropped anchor in Fremantle on Friday 17 July 1896. As the port was new there were no docks or wharves, and only the coastal passenger steamers went alongside the pier; other ships in the roads discharged into lighters. We anchored in Gage Roads on our arrival, then owing to the winter season we shortly moved to Owen's Anchorage three miles up the coast. On this occasion I witnessed the finest piece of

seamanship under canvas that I ever saw in my life. It was when we proceeded under sail to the anchorage where the ships were moored in tiers, the Aussie pilot was extremely skilful in handling the ship between the tiers making a perfect running moor.
Discharging was a problem because there were more ships than lighters, consequently, great competition for preference ensued between captains. It was then that I appreciated sailing a small boat as a boy. The anchorage was over three miles from the landing stage, and that would have been a long pull under oars: all ships therefore had sailing boats. I was given charge of our boat with an ordinary seaman who'd once been a fisherman. We had a fine carvel built cutter in the ship, but she'd been neglected in having been exposed to the sun for many months, and despite the carpenter's best efforts she leaked like a basket. Therefore, we had to use the ship's gig which the carpenter fitted with a false keel, the cutter's gaff boom mainsail with its jib was also used; by this means she carried too much sail and would require careful handling.
Another problem which confronted us was watering the ship as there was no water boat at the port. This task had to be carried out by filling up the casks and beakers from a tap on the jetty: then transporting them between the thwarts of the gig on sailing back to the ship. Some of the regular traders like the ***Arabella*** had a properly fitted sailing boat and a 100 gallon tank. Our procedure was to man the boat at 6 am, then bring one load of water before breakfast. After our morning meal, we would take the captain ashore then queue up with all the other boats at the only tap on the jetty. It was a contented queue and we didn't mind waiting, those at the tail end would sometimes go into town for an hour or so.
Fortunately, it was a 'soldiers wind' along the coast back to the ship, and the long narrow gig made good time under such conditions. On arrival at the ship, the barrels of water had to be hoisted aboard and emptied into the tanks; we would then proceed for another load. In the meantime however, the remainder of the crew were discharging the cargo of dressed timber with the hand winch, otherwise, they would have been carrying out maintenance work. We had many happy days in the boats often having races with each other.
Our routine was often varied by unexpected incidents. On one occasion after taking the liberty men ashore on a Saturday afternoon, the second mate from the ***Arabella*** approached me saying his boat had been stolen. We took him and his apprentice aboard our gig and pulled off in the only direction the stolen boat could have gone. Quite soon we sighted the stolen cutter making slow progress under sail. After pulling alongside, the second mate and my seaman jumped aboard and a free for all with the four pirates followed. Our fellows were having a bad time of it, so I jumped aboard with the oak tiller in my hand and succeeded in felling two of them. After overpowering the thieves, we made back to the jetty where the miscreants were handed over to the water police.
Owing to the shortage of lighters the process of discharging cargo was extremely slow:

three months passed before the operation was completed, and a stiffening of 100 tons of sand ballast was loaded. We then proceeded to a sandy bay of an uninhabited island which was known as 'Careening Bay'. This was some seven or eight miles from Owen's Anchorage. We carried on board some photographers who were making an illustrated publication on the prehistoric method of how a ship is ballasted. The morning after our arrival, the captain, second mate, carpenter and some of the hands went ashore and built a jetty on the beach. We had towed a small lighter across with shovels and wheelbarrows from Owen's Anchorage, then after heaving the ship's stern close to the beach and rigging a warp to the shore, the ballasting began. A number of the sailors were sent ashore with the shovels and wheelbarrows; two sailors manned the lighter and two more the lifeboat, this was to ferry the sand to the ship. It was then hoisted aboard with the hand dolly winch and sent down into the hold; we averaged 30 to 40 tons a day. Shortly before sailing the captain came aboard with a party of sightseers who showed great interest in the sailors singing their sea shanties as they hauled the anchors in. Sailing around to Gage Roads we anchored and prepared the ship for sea. By this time a number of the sailors had deserted for the Goolgardie Goldfields and there was a delay in obtaining replacements. One of the new sailors was a cockney named Tom Ball, a pugilist of some renown and one who caused great consternation amongst the ship's company. We eventually sailed from Fremantle after a stay of three months and 20 days; our destination was Diamond Isle in Burma for orders.

On passage through the Indian Ocean, Tom Ball who had two pairs of boxing gloves kept fit by running around the deck then boxing with some of the crew. I became one of his sparring partners; although on our first session he gave me a good hiding. However it was from this that I learned a great deal of the art. He was of extraordinary physique being about five feet eight tall, stockily built with a 44 inch chest. He'd been born in a travelling caravan, and taught as a youth to box at country fairs. He soon established himself as the cock of the foc'sle.

Tom Ball had to be taken out of the second mate's watch and transferred to the mates, as it appeared as though he wanted to take charge. He had a second mate's certificate although it was under another name; apparently he'd won it in a gambling game at Rio de Janeiro where he said he'd once been in command of a tug. However, he was a most versatile fellow, extremely good natured, and one who had always lived by his wits to a great deal.

One day in the Bay of Bengal we were becalmed and noticed a couple of turtles floating on the water. The captain ordered the gig boat away, and with muffled oars approached a large slumbering turtle stern first. Tom Ball manoeuvered cautiously, leaned over and grabbed the turtle by its hind flippers, then with the aid of a rope hauled it aboard the gig and turned the turtle on its back. The turtle had a powerful jaw which was quite capable of taking a mans hand off, however, once on its back it was helpless. When the cook had decapitated the creature, all hands had turtle soup for many days, we also enjoyed the steaks from it. On arrival at Diamond Island we found scores of turtle eggs which were round in shape but made good eating.

In due course, orders were received for Calcutta to load gunny bags for the west coast of South America. When we arrived at Princeps Ghat, Ball, through the newspaper offered to fight any man in India; his challenge was taken up by an Army boxer. Ball promptly went into training with his record of sparring being published in The Times of India. Unfortunately, the fight which was to have taken place in 'The Maidan' did not come off. Tom Ball's opponent who'd no doubt been reading the newspaper reports, withdrew from the contest and forfeited his stake. This was a great disappointment to the ship's company, as we wanted to see what kind of a show Ball was able to put up against someone of his own calibre. On another occasion when sitting in the courtyard lounge of a Calcutta hotel, he overheard a conversation between the captain of a Clan Line steamer and his companion. He was a big man boasting of his large hands and his ability to spread his fingers further than any of his friends: Ball interrupted and offered to take up the challenge. After some discussion it was agreed they should spread their hands between two glasses on the table; Ball then suggested a wager. The captain suggested 15 rupees, Ball laughed and bluffed the figure to 60 rupees. The captain agreed then spread the glasses with his fingers; but Ball spread them much further, and in doing so even knocked one of the glasses off the table. After another heated discussion Tom Ball walked away with his 60 rupees.

Before leaving Calcutta the captain paid Ball off at his own request, and due to his dominating personality the ship's company were greatly relieved by his departure. After an enjoyable stay at the Indian port where we were entertained by many friends, we completed loading and sailed on 2 February 1897. After dropping down to Garden Reach, the tug ***Rescue*** took us in tow down the River Hoogley during which time, we saw the wreck of the steamer ***Canterbury*** on the James and Mary Shoal. Anchoring at Jellingham Roads for the night, we proceeded down river past Sauger Island, then dropped the pilot and headed for the open sea.

Going down the Bay of Bengal and nearing the equator we experienced the tail end of a cyclone which reduced the ship to two lower topsails, fore topmast and mizzen staysails. When going aloft the rain was so heavy it was like climbing with a bag of coal on one's back. On this occasion our Scottish captain served out a tot of whisky to all hands from his own stock; this gave us the impression we were in for a really bad time with the weather. Sailing east we crossed the International Date Line after 69 days, an occasion on which, we were served with the traditional double helping of pea soup. The passage to Valparaiso

was completed on May 19 after a run of 104 days.
Shortly after our arrival at the Chilean port we experienced a 'Norther'; these are gales which are most prevalent during the winter months. Ships are moored in tiers with both bower anchors out, six shackles of cable on one, and seven on the other as well as the kedge anchor. During these 'Northers' the full force of the wind isn't felt because of the backdrop of the Andes Mountains surmounted by the high peak of Aconcagua. However, the sea rolled in with a tremendous swell which necessitated good ground tackle to withstand the heavy strain on the anchor cables. Our captain was an experienced seaman and took every precaution: the upper yards were sent down, the t'gallant masts housed, and springs placed on the anchor cables. The 15 inch coir towing hawser was taken right aft to the bitts, both ends were then brought forward, and made fast to the anchor cable foreside of the windlass under the foc'sle head. A double luff tackle was attached to the towing hawser on each side amidships, and led to the main capstan to take the strain off the windlass.
During the worst of the hurricane all hands were ordered aft to the safety of the poop, and although the ship was comparatively light she still dipped her foc'sle head right under the huge rolling seas of the Pacific Ocean. As the ***Aethelbert*** lifted her bows and the cables tautened, the coir towing hawser took the strain and stretched to almost twice its normal length, this took the strain off the anchor cables and prevented the sudden jerk which would have taken place. One of the other ships sent up distress signals, the lifeboat then came out and stood by her all night; the vessel in distress wasn't many cable lengths away from the rocks. Fortunately we rode out the weather with just one of our cables parting.
After we'd discharged part of the cargo we proceeded to Tocapilla, Iquique, Caleta Buena, then Junin where we loaded saltpetre.
The west coast of South America lacked lighthouses and other navigational aids: on account of the Humboldt Current setting to the northward, ships had to be careful not to be carried north of their destination. On this occasion when making Tocapilla, we closed the land as our captain assumed the port was right ahead; we then saw a pilot boat under four oars and preparations were made for entering harbour. When our captain hailed the pilot it was only then that he realised he was a long way off his destination, and all due to the Humboldt Current. My four years of apprenticeship was completed while we were at Junin, and after a discussion with the captain I was transferred to the ***Jessie Osborne*** which was homeward bound; this would enable me to sit my second mates examination without wasting too much time. The ***Aethelbert*** then sailed for Honolulu.
It was a long monotonous passage to Falmouth on the ***Jessie Osborne,*** this was largely due to the nervousness of the master who was a part owner and carried his family aboard. Each night he would shorten sail before turning in; he was so different from the type of captains

I'd previously sailed with. There was no incident worth recording on the 114 day passage except the captain's failure to take advantage of carrying sail when the opportunity arose; this was especially around Cape Horn where we had a good strong north westerly wind. When we did reach Falmouth for orders, it was to suffer the indignity of being towed to Rotterdam where the ship paid off. I later heard the captain had retired from the sea.

Photo - James Maguire

Hollinwood

A short story from William Peck who served his four years apprenticeship in sail.

In September 1895 I was sent to join the ***Hollinwood;*** at that time the vessel was loaded and laying at the North Woolwich buoys ready to sail. She was a four masted barque under the command of Captain W R Kidd, owned by MacVicar Marshall & Co and registered in Liverpool.
The vessel had been built of steel on the River Mersey by Roydens in 1889; she was 2,673 tons: length of 307 feet: beam of 45, and her depth of hold 24.2 feet.
From the River Thames we sailed in ballast to Newcastle NSW in what proved to be a smart though uneventful passage. One evening at Newcastle when I was on my way to the Seamen's Institute, I bumped into an old school chum who had in fact left home the same time as myself. I made a habit of visiting his ship, this was for a meal which was of a high standard; the ***Hollinwood*** was a hungry ship, and what little food there was wasn't very pleasing.
We loaded coal then sailed for San Francisco rounding The Kings in extremely bad weather; it was then discovered that our cargo was on fire. However, we managed to make it to Lyttleton in New Zealand arriving there on 27 December 1895. Most of the cargo was discharged to extinguish the fire, it was then reloaded in an operation which took six of the best weeks of my life. Once again the ship set sail for San Francisco, and it was during the course of this passage that we picked up the crew of the four masted barque ***Republic*** of Liverpool. She was also bound from Newcastle NSW with coal for 'Frisco. After we'd left her, she was burning from end to end in 34 N and 127 W.
During the passage I had a most embarrassing moment; in being the smallest of the apprentices, it was my job to get the bread tanks and fill the biscuit barges for the foc'sle and half-deck crowds. On one particular morning I filled the box up and was on my way to the half-deck, it was then that I noticed the head was off the sugar cask in the lazarette. I just couldn't resist and filled the box up with sugar, then covered the stolen booty with the hard tack biscuits. On reaching the deck, Captain Kidd who, like the ship, was from Liverpool, ordered me onto the poop-deck with the box; I was then told to up-end the container in order for the captain to ascertain its contents. At first I hesitated, however, when I saw the end of the gaff topsail halyard in the Old Man's hand, I speeded up his

order. The sequel was I lost my afternoon watch below for a month, and my whack of sugar was denied me for the same period.
Whilst discharging our coal cargo next to JD Spreckle's sugar refinery at San Francisco, the story of my sugar stealing escapade reached the ears of the factory foreman. He offered me a whole sack of sugar if I was able to carry it from the mill and back to the ship. The task seemed impossible. However, once it was on my shoulders, and after quite a struggle the task was completed.
During our long wait for a cargo at 'Frisco, one of the AB's fell from aloft; his fall was broken on hitting the lower shrouds before going overboard. After a period ashore in hospital, he decided to re-join the ship which was then loading grain for Hull.
After we'd been at sea for a few weeks, the same AB who had the fall from aloft at 'Frisco went sick; he was taken from the foc'sle to one of the spare staterooms where it was assumed he may find some peace and quiet to speed his recovery. In the continuing good weather, another apprentice and myself were promoted to the post of 'nurse' in order to watch over the ailing sailor. One evening during my temporary job, I'd checked the patient and made myself nice and comfortable on the settee when the Old Man walked in.
"Well how's your patient, Mr Peck?" enquired the captain
"Oh, he's sleeping peacefully sir" I replied.
The master mariner then gave the AB a closer examination.
"Sleeping peacefully indeed, Mr Peck," exclaimed Captain Kydd, "This is one sleep he's not going to wake up from."
The ***Hollinwood*** called in at the Pitcairn Islands, and from there we loaded a welcome supply of fresh fruit, vegetables, replenished our water supply, and many other things which eased the length of the passage. Our arrival at Hull was completed after 140 days.
Our next voyage was with coal to Rio de Janeiro; thence in ballast to New York. From the American port we took general cargo out to Sydney, and from there a cargo of wool, hides and copra was loaded. The ***Hollinwood*** left Australia for London on 22 May 1898; good progress was made around the Horn. However, shortly after she'd crossed the equator, fire was discovered beneath number one hatch. Consequently, as much of the affected cargo as possible was jettisoned over the wall. However, our efforts were in vain as the fire began to spread to the rest of the cargo. A week later the ship was on fire fore and aft. We signalled two ships who hardly needed any telling, and they stood by till nothing more could be done. One half of our crew went aboard the German ship ***Khorasan*** bound for the UK, whilst the remainder of the crew of which I was one, took refuge in the Cardiff registered ***Patterdale.*** The ***Khorasan*** arrived at the UK 14 days ahead of the ***Patterdale***.
After several weeks ashore, I was sent to Swansea to join the four masted barque ***Crompton*** which was another of the company's ships. Loading a cargo of coal we sailed

for 'Frisco where on arrival I left the ship, rejoicing in the fact that my term of apprenticeship was over. I was by that time thoroughly disillusioned with sail and decided to join the ***SS Morgan City;*** this steamer was on a regular run from 'Frisco to Manila with troops, nursing staff and horses. She was a great ship with a good crowd of officers; the food was really first class, something that was never found on sailing vessels. Most unfortunately the ship was wrecked in the Inland Sea whilst bound for Kobe to load coal bunkers.

The troops and nursing staff were taken off two days later, whilst the crew remained on board to assist the Japanese in an attempt to salve the vessel; our efforts were unsuccessful. Later on I contracted malaria then pleurisy, and due to my illness, I was taken to a French hospital at Nagasaki. On being discharged some weeks later, the American consul put me on board the troopship ***SS City of Ohio*** as a passenger. To relieve the monotony, I went aft one night to read the Walker's Patent Log for the mate on watch.

On the boat deck there were scores of coffins, these contained the embalmed bodies of American troops that were being transported back to the USA for burial. As I passed between the coffins and along the deck I received a kick from somewhere, after which, I made my way to the bridge at a much greater speed.

The officer on watch laughed at my supposing one of the corpses had attacked me, and when his watch was over we both went aft with a lantern to ascertain the originator of the kick. On arrival we found a soldier wrapped in a blanket asleep amongst the coffins, he'd decided to sleep on deck as it was too hot in the accommodation.

We duly arrived at 'Frisco where I met Captain A McCausland of the iron ship ***Pythomene***; he persuaded me to join his ship and travel home where I could sit my second mates certificate. On arrival at the UK I sat the examination, but most unfortunately I failed the eyesight test and also my ticket, I then gave up the sea for a good job ashore. However the call back to the sea was strong and I made a return in 1915. After three years of the Great War I was torpedoed in 1918, as a result of my injuries I am now an invalid-chair sailor.

Dalgonar

By Captain Joseph Kay

Over the centuries there have been so many sailing ships in existence, that any one particular vessel would hardly have come to notice - unless of course, something spectacular had happened to that ship! Quite often one ship has performed some feat outside the realms of normality placing her in the annals of maritime history. The Liverpool registered ***Dalgonar*** was one such ship.

Built for Gracie Beazley of Liverpool and coming from Oswald & Mordaunts Southampton yard, the ***Dalgonar*** was launched in January 1892. Her main asset, like so many other windjammers of the day, was she could carry a large cargo of over 4,000 tons with a comparatively small crew. However, it needed a gale of wind on either quarter to get 10 knots out of her. She was indeed one of those clumsy unhandy ships, which as previously mentioned, were built by the mile and sawn off into lengths.

Built of steel, the dimensions of ***Dalgonar*** were 296 bp x 42.3 x 25.2 feet, she had steel pole masts with wooden t'gallants and royals; her sail plan was normal in having split topsails, but on the mainmast, as well as the split topsail, the t'gallant sail was also split; furthermore, and although obsolete at the time, she had reef points in her courses and upper topsails.

As was common the officers and steward lived aft, whilst the rest of the crew were accommodated forward. The sailor's foc'sle was a large steel deckhouse abaft the foremast; the galley and donkey boiler were situated at the after end of that structure. The steering position was aft on a whaleback stern, whilst on the forward end of the poop deck was a chartroom. ***Dalgonar*** had a light grey hull, black topsides, 13 painted gunports on a broad white band to compliment a red boot topping. Beneath her steel bowsprit, was a gold and white figurehead of a lady pointing the way ahead. The ship's building costs were £23,361.

On 11 February 1892, whilst under the command of Captain John Gray, the new ship was towed from Southampton to Barry where she loaded a cargo of coke for Port Pirie. Beginning her maiden voyage on 21 March 1892, she arrived at her destination on July 14, then in continuance of the trip, loaded coal at Newcastle NSW for San Diego. ***Dalgonar*** then went in ballast to Tacoma to load a grain cargo for Liverpool. The ship's

maiden voyage of 16 months ended at the Herculaneum Dock on 27 July 1893.
The next voyage began on 9 September 1893 when she took a full cargo of salt from Liverpool to Calcutta. The homeward passage was a 4,000 ton cargo of linseed. After a long passage of 162 days from Calcutta, ***Dalgonar*** arrived at Hull.
Captain James Kitchen then took command. The next voyage was from Hull to New York, but in strong headwinds that passage took 50 days. The ship then loaded case oil for Yokahama. However, an incident of note occurred on that voyage, when after having left New York and being 15 days out, fire was discovered in the paint locker. After fighting the blaze for an hour or so, the danger was eliminated and normality resumed. The passage took 131 days. After loading a full cargo at Yokohama for Tacoma, the ***Dalgonar*** took 39 days to cross the Pacific, and once there she loaded a cargo of wheat for Liverpool. The first three voyages of the ***Dalgonar*** had gone very well, but the fourth was full of excitement, and this unpleasant trip is described by one of her Liverpool sailors. Quote.
"I signed on the ***Dalgonar*** on 27 June 1896 and we were loaded for Sydney with a general cargo. This consisted of barbed wire, crockery, paint, sheep dip, oakum, and various other articles for the colonies. To liven things up a bit, we also had 20 tons of gunpowder in the 'tween decks beneath the after hatch. I was in the second mate's watch, and when we were 15 days out, I was watch below when things really livened up.
One of the men in the mate's watch was working up aloft, and whilst at the main crosstrees he suddenly noticed a thin wisp of smoke coming from the top of the steel pole mast... Fire! Instead of coming to the deck down the ratlines to raise the alarm, he slid down the t'gallant backstay. Then with his excellent vocal chords, excitedly let everyone on board know there was a fire in the hold.
Everybody in the ship knew there was gunpowder amongst the cargo, and indeed, the crowds response to the alarm was lightning quick. In a very short space of time, and without waiting to be ordered by captain or mate, the after hatch was stripped to reveal the thick black smoke pouring out. Without any telling some of the hands went below, A chain gang was formed and the 20 tons of explosives were jettisoned over the wall in record time.
Ships of sail like the ***Dalgonar*** were without bulkheads and only had one big hold. With the wind being on the quarter, the fore hatch was then opened to allow the smoke to be blown right through and escape at the other end. Whilst the explosives were being thrown overboard, a boat towing astern was made ready fully laden with provisions; then just in case! the other boats were swung out in their davits.
When the last case of the gunpowder had gone over, the hatches were battened down and the donkey engine started. The ship had a two and a half inch pipe that ran under the top

rail, and from this couplings were spaced 20 feet apart. On these couplings ... or fire hydrants - hoses to fight a fire could be connected. The chippy was then given the job of cutting through the wooden deck to allow a steam hose to be inserted into the hold, however, he couldn't get through the steel deck beneath the wooden decking. Old Captain Kitchen said he thought he could make St.Vincent that night, but on seeing the palls of smoke from our ship, a steamer came to the rescue; I think she was one of Houstons. Standing by us all night the steamer's captain offered to take us all off and let the ship burn; but when morning broke the Old Man thanked him and away he went.
The following day we started getting the cable up from the locker. A sailor went down to hitch a rope on to the cable, but just as he'd made it fast he dropped unconscious. Another sailor went down with a bowline around himself to rescue him, but as soon as he'd secured his fallen shipmate he dropped as well. With lines already around both men, they were hauled up and laid out on deck where after some time they both recovered. The fumes from the sheep dip in the cargo had turned into a poisonous gas, and almost finished the pair of them off. Two days later the ship made St Vincent with the fire in the hold still burning. We then started the donkey boiler to force steam into the hold. The captain hired lighters and barges, and as soon as they were alongside we started discharging cargo into them. However, the local natives who worked the barges wouldn't go into the hold. With the fire still going on, we had to go down below in the smoke filled hold, where we worked for about an hour at a time, but as soon as we came back up and climbed over the hatch coaming, each man went down in a fit when the fresh air hit him."
After about 3 weeks the fire was eventually exinguished, and the tug ***Blazer*** rather belatedly arrived from Liverpool ... with a couple of fire pumps on board. In re-stowing the cargo from the lighters, much of the 'tween deck cargo was stowed in the lower hold to stiffen her a bit. The t'gallants and their yards were sent down from each mast, then with the ***Blazer*** in charge, the long haul back to Liverpool began; the tow started on 11 August 1896. After six days we made Funchal in Madeira then left the next day. Unfortunately we had a lot of headwinds from there, and due to this, the ***Dalgonar*** could only assist the tow with a staysail from time to time. Reaching Liverpool on September 7 we went through the Wapping, then into the Albert dock - otherwise known as the pawnshop.
After discharging, the ship was given a full refit before resuming her voyage to Sydney - a trip that began on 28 Nov 1896. In the Bay of Biscay heavy weather was experienced, and during that blow we lost the fore t'gallant as well as some sails. On New Years Day 1897, Captain Kitchen asked the ***SS Zero*** to report him damaged. However, after a passage of 116 days the ***Dalgonar*** arrived in Port Jackson on 27 March 1897. Captain Kitchen who'd always been popular with his crews had been in the ship for six and a half years, however, in March 1900 on the ***Dalgonar's*** arrival in London, he retired from the

1892 *Dalgonar* 1914

Liverpool County Museum

Without a breath of wind to fill her sails, the *Dalgonar* is stopped dead in the water. In conditions such as this when not making any way, the ship can't be steered and will drift lazily around the ocean.
The picture on the left shows there is nobody at the helm.
When in the Atlantic Ocean near the equator, ships in such situations of being without wind are said to be caught in the doldrums. They can be trapped there for weeks, or even months, and quite often run out of food and more importantly … water.
The term doldrums is also referred to as the 'Horse Latitudes.' Supposedly named because when sailing ships were carrying horses across the Atlantic, and after being caught in the doldrums, the animals had to be put down through lack of drinking water.

sea. Spending the rest of his life at his home in Hoylake, Captain Kitchen died in 1925. Command of the vessel then went to Captain Isbister, a man who proved to be equally respected by all who sailed under him. Captain Isbister was to stay in the ***Dalgonar*** for the next thirteen and a half years and was to be her last captain.

During the time Captain Isbister was in the ship, he proved to be the longest serving member of all the crews the ship ever had, and indeed, his travels in the vessel took him far and wide. In his ten voyages as captain of the ***Dalgonar,*** a full list of all the ports he'd sailed to, began from London where he took command in March 1890.

London to Sydney, Newcastle NSW, Tocopilla, Falmouth, Hamburg.

Sydney, Falmouth, Liverpool.

Sydney, Newcastle NSW, San Francisco, Liverpool.

Sydney, Newcastle NSW, Coquimbo, Antofagasta, Plymouth, Antwerp.

Valparaiso, Iquique, Antofagasta, Rotterdam, Hamburg.

Astoria, Dublin, Liverpool.

Sydney, Newcastle NSW, Coquimbo, Talcahuano, Queenstown, Hull, South Shields.

Seattle, Queenstown, Rochefort, Liverpool.

Sydney, Newcastle NSW, Coquimbo, Taltal, Dunkirk, London.

During Captain Isbister's command of the *Dalgonar* where he ran a good ship, he'd also had his fair share of dangers and mishaps. However, when the *Dalgonar* left London on 12 Nov 1912, it was to be her last voyage, a voyage that would place her firmly in the record books.

Sailing for Melbourne, the *Dalgonar* with her cargo of cement and general arrived after a 105 days run. After discharging she went around to Newcastle and loaded coal for Callao, a port she arrived at after being 53 days at sea. On discharging the ship was ballasted with shingle, and on 24 September 1913 set sail for Taltal. The distance between the ports is about 650 miles, and Captain Isbister no doubt thought he'd get there quite comfortably in 4 or 5 days. But it was not to be - for the ship ran into a cyclone! ***Dalgonar*** had seen it all before, but except for the bare minimum of ballast the hold was empty. In the mountainous seas the unstable ship pitched and rolled wildly. Then after her sails were blown out she couldn't be steered or sailed and was driven far from her course. On October 9, the ballast which had not been boxed off properly, shifted to port and the ***Dalgonar*** lay on her beam ends. In an attempt to relieve the ship, Captain Isbister ordered the masts to be cut away. Amidst the raging winds and mountainous seas, the starboard shrouds and backstays were released allowing the masts to go over the port side, but this act only exacerbated the problem. The tangled mass of wire and masts were still connected to the ship by the port shrouds, and this heeled the vessel over even more. The terrible mess of what was once the ship's top hamper was now ranging up and down, threatening at any moment to pierce the ship's side. Captain Isbister knew only too well that if this did happen, the ship would go down like a stone. In the ever vicious weather when it appeared as though the ship was going to founder, the captain on seeing there was no hope ordered all hands to abandon ship. Whilst giving assistance in swinging the lee side boat out, the captain was swept off his feet by the seas and lay badly injured. Then before he could be helped, the captain was washed overboard never to be seen again. The lee side boat was crushed. Three sailors were also lost in the attempted launch of the starboard boat, the remainder of the boat's crew then climbed back aboard, where they and the rest of their shipmates sought the sanctuary of the 'tween deck. Here they stayed barely clad but survived on hard tack and bracken water. On October 10, the day after the crowd had taken refuge in the 'tween deck, the French four masted barque ***Loire*** - Captain Michel Jaffre, arrived on the scene under lower topsails; after observing and ascertaining there was life on board the mast-less ship, the Frenchman hove to for a rescue attempt. The weather was far too bad to even think of putting one of his boats down, but the gallant Frenchman stood by for three days in the mountainous seas awaiting his chance. During that three days, in both the torrential rain and darkness, the ***Loire*** lost sight of the ***Dalgonar*** on a number of occasions. During this time however, an attempt was made by some of the ***Dalgonar's*** crew to relieve the ship by cutting away as much of the rig as possible; they knew it was a pocket of air in the hold that was keeping their ship afloat, they also knew if one of those huge spars punctured the hull, all would be lost.

Amidst the continuing storm, the port side of the ***Dalgonar's*** deck was completely under water. Cutting away some of the rigging relieved this to some degree but the list remained. Captain Jaffre later said he was apprehensive of getting too close to the stricken ***Dalgonar,*** this was because of a possible collision in the huge seas. However, on October 13, when the weather subsided to a gale the Frenchman began his gallant rescue.

It was Yves Cadic the first mate of the *Loire*, who with eight oarsmen, took one of ***Loire's*** boats across to the ***Dalgonar.*** Contact could not at first be made, as the boat was swept away each time it got into a favourable position. Fortunately, ***Dalgonar's*** chippy Mr Dunker, had made a number of cane fenders which at the time were in the 'tween deck. One of these was made fast to a line, floated downwind and grasped by the rescuers with a boat hook. Then after great difficulty which took all day, 13 crew men from the ***Dalgonar*** were taken on board the ***Loire*** before the remaining 13 were taken off.

The position given for the rescue was 26S - 130W, but the abandoned ship refused to sink. Because of the pocket of air in her hold, and after a six months drift, it is estimated that ***Dalgonar*** drifted between 4,000 and 5,000 miles before piling up on Mopihaa Island. During her long drift, she was seen and reported as a derelict hulk by the French barque ***Marie*** on December 10. On 4 February 1914 in a position of 26S 122W, she was boarded by a party from the American five masted schooner ***Inca,*** who then salvaged anything of value. Amongst the articles taken were Captain Isbister's 2 chronometers, his sextant, and the binnacle. Although it was still possible to salvage the ship with a tug, the ship which refused to sink was allowed to drift to her final resting place. That place was made in March 1914.

The fact that the ***Loire's*** captain stood by as he did in the hurricane, proves that despite all the squabbling amongst politicians ... who never dirty their hands, that there is no divide between seamen of any nation, and each will risk his life for the other.

Monsieur Yves Cadic the first mate of the ***Loire***, suffered cold and exhaustion after his heroic rescue and was laid up. Because of this, he later developed bronchitis followed by pneumonia and died at sea a short time later.

The ***Loire*** was the penultimate sailing ship to be built for the famous shipping firm of Anton Bordes. She was launched at Nantes in 1897, and as some of her passages show, she proved to be a very fast ship; many times she logged over 17 knots for the whole of a four hour watch, and on numerous occasions over 350 miles a day. One point of note however, is during the First World War when the Frenchman was ordered by a German armed merchantman to heave to instead, ***Loire's*** captain crowded on all sail. The warship then fired a shot bringing her fore topmast down before calling the action off. However, and even without her fore topmast, ***Loire*** soon left the steamer far astern.

Some of the ***Loire's*** passages in her first 6 years have been recorded as follows.

1897 - Portland to Iquique 66 days
1897 Iquique - Prawle Point 75 days
1898 - Beachy Head to Valparaiso 69 days
1899 - Iquique to Gravelines 79 days
1900 - Dunkirk to Iquique - 75 days
1901 - Antwerp to Iquique 72 days
1901 - Iquique to Prawle point 86 days
1902 - Isle of Wight to Iquique 85 days
1903 - Iquique to Lizard 80 days

The law of the sea stipulates that abandoned ships can be possessed, salvaged or stripped. On finding the *Dalgonar* abandoned, the captain of the American schooner *Inca,* quite rightfully took anything of value from the abandoned hulk.. Below— The fogbound *Dalgonar.*

Author's Collection

Lawhill

Arranmore

Birkdale

California

Holkar

Kathleen and May

Kathleen and May

Liverpool

Sindia

Wavertree

Andora

From Sea Breezes by Captain FJ Thomson whose last ship was the Aethelbert.

After having passed my second mates examination and on taking a spot of leave, I obtained the appointment of second mate on the ***Andora.*** This full rigged ship belonged to EF&W Roberts of Liverpool, and she was bound from her home port to load a general cargo in New York for Melbourne. The master was an entirely different type from the last one I'd sailed with on the ***Jessie Osborne,*** and was perhaps, the greatest captain under whom I was ever to serve; indeed, a Bluenose who'd been brought up in the 'hard school.' In his early days he'd worked in his grandfather's shipyard where they'd built wooden ships. It has been said by many, that those hardy seamen could build a ship, make the spars and sails, then sail her around the world.

Most certainly, Captain Davis of the ***Andora*** was a smarter carpenter than the ship's own; he could also teach the sail-maker a few things he'd never heard of. The first mate was a young man who'd gone to sea at the age of 14. He'd sailed with our Nova Scotia captain before, and when just 20 years old, became first mate of the ***Andora*** a 1,800 ton main skysail full rigger.

We carried a real hard case Liverpool crew, and with the ship being in ballast, the passage across the North Atlantic was one to be remembered. In those days discipline was maintained chiefly by the forceful personality of the captain and his mates; in this case it was with the addition of the bosun who'd previously been an apprentice. The only other member of the after guard was the 70 year old steward.

Andora was indeed a hungry ship. This point was well illustrated when just one case of condensed milk containing 12 tins, had been supplied for a voyage of probably 18 months. That milk was for cabin use only ... there was none for the sailors. On one occasion when the mate and I were at breakfast, he held up the milk jug and called into the pantry. "Steward." On the old gentleman's arrival, the mate inquired.

"What d'you call this?" To which he received the reply.

"Milk sir." To which the mate declared.

"Milk, dammit. I'd be able to see the bottom in seven fathoms of the stuff."

The inference being that the milk was extremely watery.

As a passenger for the outward trip to Melbourne, we had a 17 year old youth named Douglas Bannatyne. His father was a marine insurance broker, and he'd sent him forth to gain some knowledge of ships and shipping. His itinerary was to travel out to Australia by sail then return home on a steamer. As he played the violin and I could strum a banjo, we had many a pleasant evening together during the dog watches. Indeed, it was during one of our dog watch discussions, that I learned we had other things in common. He was a keen yachtsman and had handled eighteen-footers on the River Mersey; in the very same races that I'd also taken part.

We beat across the North Atlantic in ballast, frequently taking long reaches and often wearing ship. Eventually, we arrived at New York on a Sunday morning after a 42 day passage. Before the sails were furled however, two smart four oared boats pulled alongside. Their crews then threw hooks over the rail, swarmed aboard, then went aloft to help the sailors stow sail. This looked very ominous! On coming down to the deck the uninvited boarders went into the foc'sle with the sailors; they then plied them with rum and told them to pack their bags.

The mate saw what was happening and reported to the captain, the three of us then went forrard to see what was afoot. Meanwhile, the leader of the gang was sitting on the top-rail above his boat; he was hailed by Captain Davis who protested at his attempt to steal his crew, even before getting the ship alongside. The gang leader tapped his revolver in his hip pocket and replied.

"Guess we're just going to take them captain, although I'll leave you one as a watchman."

I ran aft and hoisted the ensign upside down for assistance, however, nobody took the slightest bit of notice. The Liverpool sailors departed with their gear into the two boats, and this was just a few cable-lengths from the Statue of Liberty.

After loading had been completed at Brooklyn, a new crowd of sailors were brought along at the very last minute by the boarding-house master, and what a motley lot they were, we later learned that some of them had never even been to sea before. Running her easting down in the Roaring Forties, some good day to day runs and the ***Andora*** was made to show her paces. On one occasion, we were running before a stiff westerly gale under reefed fore-course and topsails, the sky was black with heavy squalls rising from the west. However, when the second dog watch was over the barometer began rising and the reefs were shaken out; we were simply reeling off the knots.

At midnight the captain was convinced the barometer was rising further and thought the worst was over, then in the moderating wind he gave the order to hoist the main t'gallant sail. It was a real surprise for the men to perform such a duty in the middle watch, this was a job for all hands, and it was only with great difficulty that the yard was eventually hoisted.

After seeing the sail set, the Old Man who'd been on the poop-deck for at least 24 hours went below, he left me in charge saying the wind was beginning to lose its kick. Half an hour later an ominous black cloud came up from the westward and I just hoped the Old Man's forecast had been a good one. As a first trip second mate it was quite a thrilling moment when the squall struck with a tremendous force. Any attempt to take in the main t'gallant would have resulted in losing it; there was nothing to be done except watch the steering and see the squall through. The ship which shortly before had been rolling quite heavily and shipping a great deal of water, suddenly steadied herself and fairly skimmed over the seas without a roll.

At that particular time, the watch were all on the poop where they thought they'd be safer. However, with the ship racing through the seas in what must have been her optimum speed, some of them looked rather frightened. I ordered the log to be streamed and the line ran out to a clinch, this indicated the ship was making at least 14 knots. There were further squalls during my watch although there wasn't much in them, this made me realise that the captain's forecast had been correct even if a little premature. We made a good passage to Melbourne, by which time our new 'sailors' had been knocked into shape.

On reaching Melbourne I had a picture of the ship painted by a visiting marine artist. It illustrated the moon just showing over a cloud bank. Most unfortunately, and at a later date during the First World War, it 'disappeared' whilst my furniture was being stored.

After discharge the ship loaded for Mauritius then sailed in ballast to Newcastle NSW. Many of the crew had contracted malaria at Mauritius, a fact that was notable in our passage back across the Indian Ocean. The disease spread rapidly through the ship. All hands were affected except for one ordinary seaman and myself. There were several deaths and one of them was the bosun's mate, an old German who'd once held command. This man who was six feet tall was either the second or third to be buried. At breakfast time, it was the captain who raised the issue of 'why should sailors always be buried sewn up in canvas? Therefore, a coffin was made for the bosun's mate. It had a 12 inch compartment at the lower end, and in this was a length of chain to sink the coffin. A coffin that was now over seven feet in length.

The funeral took place with all hands present, the ship was becalmed and rolling on the ocean swell. As was customary, the coffin was placed on a plank, draped with the red ensign, then confined to the sea. As expected it went down feet first, then as the sailors were watching over the gun whale it shot up again almost coming back on board again. This was because the coffin never had enough air holes in it to make it sink; it was floating head end up with about a quarter of it above the surface. The ship was completely stationary and the holds were empty, the coffin bumped against the ship's side, and the sounds echoed eerily through the ship. After drifting round to the stern, it then bobbed

around to the other side before eventually sinking. The sailors took this to be an ill omen, and especially when shortly afterwards the wind came whistling through the rigging. However, we reached Newcastle without any further ado and loaded coal for the WCSA. This was to be my first experience of a coal cargo.
After an uneventful passage across the Pacific, the ship discharged at Iquique; orders were then given to load saltpetre and proceed to Falmouth for orders. It was during this passage and whilst rounding Cape Horn, that I developed a severe attack of rheumatism in my right ankle and left knee. This affliction left me as a passenger for the rest of the voyage. For several weeks I was unable to move from my bunk, and as it was towards the end of an 18 month voyage in an ill found hungry ship, the medicine chest was empty. This had not been replenished after the malaria epidemic which had swept the ship. The lack of replacement medical aid had been blamed on the high cost of drugs and medicines in South America. Consequently, I received little medical attention apart from the steward who kindly massaged me with liniment oil. It was extremely painful, and was afterwards described by a doctor as the worst possible kind of treatment. He said wrapping the affected areas in cotton wool and keeping them warm constituted the required cure. Medical opinion was I'd suffered a severe attack of rheumatic fever.
We also ran out of food, and this resulted in all hands being placed on half rations in the North Atlantic. Fortunately, we sighted a Lamport and Holt steamer and obtained supplies from her. I'd lost so much weight in this homeward passage, and I overheard the captain despairing of ever getting me home. However, a strong constitution stood the strain and I was landed at Falmouth. I was by then a skeleton of my former self, and my clothes hung off me as though I was a scarecrow. After treatment at home I went to the brine baths at Droitwich and spent my convalescence at Harrogate. When I'd recovered completely, I sat my first mates examination, and on hearing I'd been successful, I gave up sail and went into steam.

Lonsdale

From Sea Breezes by Capt. AH Miller

In April 1896 I was sent to Hamburg to join the Liverpool ship ***Lonsdale***. She was a three masted full rigger belonging to Peter Iredale & Porter, otherwise known as the Dale Line. I was 14 years old at the time, and my father had paid 30 guineas for my apprenticeship of four and a half years 'tuition.' Commanded by Captain J Frazer the ship was 1,685 tons and built of steel with an iron deck; there were no freeing ports just scupper ways, and because of this, as I was soon to discover she was an extremely wet ship.
At the time of my signing on, the ship was discharging nitrates from South America, then as soon as the holds had been emptied, a full cargo of coke was loaded for the smelting works of Port Pirie. A good crew of Scandinavian sailors were signed on, and not long afterwards we were heading down the River Elbe, out into the North Sea and down the English Channel. Our quarters were on the starboard side at the forward end of the poop deck, its entry was through a scuttle hatch on the fore side of the mizzen mast, and in that half-deck there were six bunks.
Food was coarse and meager. It comprised of salt pork one day, followed by salt beef the next, on Fridays when it was Catholic Day, salt fish was the fare, then on Saturday it was rice and molasses. Sunday's meal, if the cook had the ingredients to make it - and if he was in a good mood! was generally 'Harriet Lane' made into a sea pie; then there were the good old Liverpool pantiles. The weekly stores consisted of 16oz of sugar (less 2oz for sweetening the lime juice) 5oz of margarine and 11oz of marmalade, the latter of which was usually fermenting by the time of issue. The breakfast beverage was allegedly coffee ... brought from the galley in the same container in which the tea was made
In the deckhouse amidships there was a steam winch and a vertical donkey boiler; we were all under strict orders never to allow its pressure to exceed 30 pounds. However, I was unaware of this order, and one day when I was acting donkeyman, I fired up until the pressure gauge read 60; then from my excited shipmates I was hurriedly reminded of my folly.
After working our way through the trades we hit a Pampero off the River Plate, this was the cause of our losing a good deal of our fair weather sails, otherwise the passage out to Port Pirie was uneventful. The ***Lonsdale*** sailed up Spencer Gulf to the outer anchorage ending an 85 day passage. The ships that were in port with us were the ***Mooltan,***

Northern Monarch, and the ***Vale of Doon.*** Port Pirie was extremely primitivc, there was just one street with the railway station at the end, a structure that was little more than a wooden hut. On Saturday nights however, there was a wagonette which would supply free transport to the bars of the driver's choice. Here the clients could drink Aussie wine to their hearts content, then wake the next morning with a terrific headache.
To discharge the cargo of coke, a gin block was secured to the main topsail yardarm, and through this a line was led to a lead block on the quay. An old horse worked the discharge using a basket that held about a quarter ton. It was the crew who worked in the hold, they filled the baskets with shovels of all shapes and sizes. The task of filling those baskets was a back breaking one indeed. The following morning an old German AB and an ordinary seaman signed on, they were replacements for the cook and a sailor who'd recently skinned out, in their departure they took their baggage and whatever else they could acquire with them. Shore labour was later employed, and these people who were experienced in their work came aboard with huge 'graipes' and soon finished the job. We cleaned the hold and found the bilges full of copper ore slag which had previously been used for ballast; this had to be picked out and it really made our fingers sore. A trunkway was then built up from the ceiling to the 'tween deck beams fore and aft on both sides; this was to strengthen the ship's hull as we were to load a cargo of sulphide ore, otherwise known as 'the devils own cargo.'
After all the deserters had been replaced at Adelaide, it was then discovered that many of these new hands had never been to sea before, nevertheless, the ship cleared for Antwerp. We rolled constantly all the way to Cape Horn, and indeed, the ship was as wet as a half-tide rock. If the ship was heeled over one way or the other under a press of sail, then the decks on the lee side would be full right up to the top rails fore and aft. The deadweight squeezed the hull, and for this reason the rigging had been screwed down two blocks with the t'gallants and backstays frapped in abaft the masts.
After arriving at the Isle of Wight, we were towed to Antwerp where the whole night was spent in trying to enter Asia Dock; it was January 1897. After we'd finished securing alongside at 8 am, the mate took us to a cafe for breakfast. We had a real feast consisting of coffee, ham and eggs. As the cargo was coming out, the rigging was gradually slackened off until the hull became normal again. We apprentices then went on leave, and it was while we were away that the ship was dry docked for a bottom scrape. On returning from our few days of rest, the ship was in the process of loading iron pipes for Yokohama. Anchored off Flushing, our captain awaited a fair wind to take us towards Lands End. Not having to wait long for a gale, we fairly flew down the English Channel, at times making 16 knots passing both sail and steam. We thought things were going well until we approached the Cape of Good Hope, then the cargo of iron pipes began to give trouble as

their shores worked loose. It always seemed to be at night when this happened, consequently, we had to go below time and again to tom them off. Finally and after experiencing many calms we entered Yokohama Roads after a 157 day passage.
The night before our arrival, I was going aloft to furl the crojack when quite suddenly I became blind. I told the Old Man who was on the poop, and he sent me below telling me it was moon blindness. The lamp was lit in the half-deck, and on realising I could once again see, I went back on deck; however, as soon as I put my head through the scuttle hatchway I went blind again. This particular complaint hardly bothered me in the high latitudes, although for some strange reason, and if ever I was near the equator it did.
The last attack I had of this complaint was in Grimsby at the end of the voyage. Whilst there I went to visit some friends, then due to another attack of blindness, they had to lead me back to the ship. Nevertheless, this was the last attack I ever had of 'moon blindness' and ever since for some mysterious reason, I've been able to read even the smallest of print without the use of spectacles.
At Yokohama the ships in port with us were the ***Howard D Troop, Hawaiian Isles,*** and the ***Lord Wolseley.*** Shore labour worked the cargo. The Japanese people were most affable and the price of goods cheap, consequently, we all enjoyed our hospitable visit there. During our stay a typhoon struck the port; we rode this with two bowers and a kedge anchor out, at the same time an American warship - a cruiser, was steaming slow ahead hove to at her moorings. However, not all the ships in port were so lucky; two German ships took to ground and the harbour itself was strewn with wreckage.
On completing our discharge, we sailed in ballast for Puget Sound passing Cape Flattery after 35 days. The tug ***Wanderer*** took us in tow as far as Esquimalt, after which the ***Lorne*** continued the tow to Port Blakely; here we discharged some ballast before proceeding to Tacoma. After anchoring and furling sail, the boarding-house master arrived. They gave the sailors a few drinks then told them to pack their bags and get into their boat; the sailors had no option as there was no law in the place. This was in November 1897 at the very height of the gold rush. The mates and boys were then left to make the ballast logs fast alongside, this was with the use of mooring chains through the scupper pipes.
The remainder of the ballast was then worked out, and the hold lined fore and aft before being covered with burlap. The ship then went alongside to load a general cargo for Durban; this consisted of wheat, flour, tinned salmon and dried fruits. A mixed crew was supplied by the crimps, however there were only a few proper sailors amongst them. We sailed in late December, and on Christmas Day we were caught in a strong gale. All went well with our new untried sailors until the ship was off Cape Horn, there we ran before a whole westerly gale and high following seas. One Sunday at about 5 pm a huge sea

pooped us; it came over the starboard quarter and pushed the steering gear box against the wheel breaking it off at the boss. Luckily the outer rim of the wheel didn't go overboard, and later on we were able to cut hatch battens into strips, using them as spokes to 'fish' the wheel together again. The teak chart house wasn't so lucky, and the structure was ripped off at its coamings; we never saw it again nor the two binnacles that went over the wall with it.

Whenever the ship fell into a trough she rolled heavily, some of the chain sheets carried away and many of the sails were ripped to ribbons. Luck was on our side however, and with what sails we had left, the ship came to wind on a port tack. During these heavy seas with the wheel double manned and both men lashed down, the only casualty was one sailor who being the weather side helmsman sustained a broken leg.

Later on after the weather had moderated, the standard compass was positioned at the wheel. Spare sails were bent on and the ship resumed her course for Durban. On recalling this passage around Cape Horn, I can honestly say, it was the worst weather I ever witnessed in 40 years at sea. We duly arrived off Port Natal and were taken in tow by the ***Sir John***; despite the battering we'd received off the Horn, our cargo was undamaged.

After discharging we loaded sand ballast and sailed for Sydney, there we were dry-docked before sailing for New Caledonia for a nickel ore cargo. Eventually the ship sailed for Glasgow, and it was during this passage in December 1898 that terribly heavy weather was experienced in the North Atlantic. Christmas Day was spent down in the hold; there we re-trimmed the cargo which had given us a dangerous list. However, we arrived at Glasgow where a new chart room was built and a whale-back apron fitted from one quarter to the other. Our next voyage was to Sydney where on arrival we saw the ***Crown of India*** being towed in dismasted. Coal was loaded at Newcastle for Callao, then after discharge and ballasting, we set a course for Lobos for a cargo of guano. In this passage Captain Fraser decided to take his ship to the leeward of the islands, however, we were beaten back and after having been posted missing, it took 33 days to make our destination. During the homeward passage to Antwerp, the Old Man had all the apprentices down in the saloon during each second dog watch. There he gave us a good drilling in seamanship using a ship's model and other implements to further our education. During these periods of instruction we had to tack, wear, box haul then club haul ship; we also had to send the masts and yards up and down, as well as being told how to use the signal book. At the end of this voyage and thanks to our captain, I passed my second mates examination at Hull in August 1900, I was then 19 years of age. I rejoined the ***Lonsdale*** at Frederikstad where the ship was loading 'weather boards' and dressed timber for Melbourne. However, and despite having passed for second mate, the owners refused to cancel my indentures. We reached Melbourne after a 90 day passage and discharged our cargo of timber in the

Swinging Basin, the ***Amulree*** and several of the 'Invers' were also there.
Here we took on a part cargo of bagged wheat as stiffening before being towed to Geelong to load a full cargo. It was there in Geelong after five years in the ship - and all under the same captain ....that I paid off the ***Lonsdale.***
Joining the steamer ***Gareloch*** of Glasgow as third mate, I quickly found the differences between sail and steam, the most outstanding of which, was working four hours on then having eight off. Due to the Boer War being in progress, the ship was loading fodder for the army horses at Port Natal. On arrival we spent 10 days at anchor before discharging at Delagoa Bay. The ***Gareloch*** then began tramping; first to Bombay in ballast, then to Kobe with cotton goods, through the Inland Sea to Moji for bunkers, then on to Manila to load for Marseilles and London. On the next voyage the ***Gareloch*** was wrecked whilst trying to enter Diego Suarez with a cargo of coal. The whole crew took passage in a French mail steamer to Mauritius, and there we stayed in the Sailor's Home before taking further passage in the ***Cawdor Castle.*** Later on we were transferred to the ***Armadale Castle*** at Durban, and it was in this ship that we came home to Southampton.
Some years later I once again saw my first ship ***Lonsdale.*** It was whilst I was serving as first mate on the ***Kilchattan,*** a ship that was bound for Norfolk Virginia and one that had to pass through the Straights of Magellan. Anchoring for the night at Punta Arenas and amidst many fond and unforgettable memories, it was there that I saw the ***Lonsdale*** serving as a hulk. In 1912 I entered the service of the Great Central Railway Co. This was a company whose ships had been taken over by the government at the outbreak of war in 1914. In February 1916 when I was master of the ***Leicester,*** the ship was mined and sunk off Dover. Alas she went down quickly with the loss of 17 lives. I was later informed that I owed my life to the good quality of a sack of self raising flour. Apparently, I'd hung onto a sack of it as I came up for the second time, and it was this that kept me afloat until I was rescued. In 1936 I left the sea to be appointed Docking Master at the port of Immingham after 40 years at sea.

Footnote. Whilst on passage from Hamburg towards Mazatlan, the *Lonsdale* **entered Port Stanley on August 29, 1909; this was to effect repairs sustained whilst attempting to round Cape Horn. However, fire broke out on the ship whilst repairs were taking place and this resulted in her being destroyed except for the hull. She was later sold as a hulk and moored at Punta Arenas.**

Nautical Terms and Phrases

There are quite a number of nautical terms which over the years have crept into, and are now part of our everyday vocabulary. Many of these nautical terms are used as expletives, they are used without their speaker knowing exactly what they mean, yet in modern prose their conversation usually makes sense. If you listen carefully to the conversations of some people, you will occasionally hear a nautical term included in their speech.

Taken Aback In a normal conversation, let us assume that a lady had told her friend she was quite 'Taken Aback' by a remark someone had made to her. The term used by the lady, probably meant she'd been caught unawares or shocked by some statement made to her; she then used the nautical term to describe her feelings. If the lady had been asked what 'Taken Aback' meant in reality, other than being shocked, she probably wouldn't have known.
The term 'Taken Aback' comes from when the wind suddenly and unexpectedly changes direction, and blows the sails the wrong way. Such a turn of events can result in a dismasting.

Feeling Under The Weather How many times have you heard an expression by somebody saying they're feeling under the weather? No doubt that person isn't feeling in the best of health which may prevent him from performing his work. The term originally arose from the times when a ship of sail was fighting the elements and couldn't make progress due to adverse weather conditions. The ship was then said to be 'Under the Weather.'

Setting Sail One often hears of a ship which may be an aircraft carrier or possibly a passenger liner which is due to set sail for some destination or other. In reality - only a vessel with sails can actually 'Set Sail.' Nevertheless, the saying which has been with us for hundreds of years is still used to describe any vessel leaving port.

Posh Another word often used in our everyday talk, is that of 'Posh.' It is in fact an abbreviation made into a word, and this slang term stems from the sailing days of the East Indiamen. The word was then - just as it is today, used to describe a person of high social standing. In those long gone days, passengers embarking on a passage to India were graded into classes of first, second, or steerage. In order to have the sunny side of the ship, the first class passengers would be accommodated on the port side of the ship whilst on its outward passage to India. This would mean, that as the ship sailed down the Atlantic and as far as Cape Town, those first class passengers would have the morning sun on the port side as it rose in the east.
On the return passage from India, the first class passengers would have their cabins or staterooms on the starboard or opposite side of the vessel. This accommodation move as the ship travelled northwards up the Atlantic, would ensure that the first class passengers would again have the benefit of the morning sun. Those first class passengers were known as 'Port Out Starboard Home' or in an abbreviation POSH.

Well Heeled This term - another way of describing a 'Posh' person, is often used to identify someone who is financially well off, well dressed and making good progress through life. Although it is hard to find a similarity in both phrases, it has the same meaning as a ship making good progress through the water in being well heeled. In such conditions, a 'Well Heeled' ship is listed over under a good press of wind on her sails and making good progress.

Hard Up This term usually implies that its speaker is devoid or rather low on finances with nothing to spare. The nautical term has many definitions, some of which, are when the wheel is hard up, the yards are braced hard up, or when two blocks are rove hard up; just like the 'Hard Up' person, there is no extra - nothing to spare.

Bearing Up Another term often used, and one from a person who may be suffering some hardship and coming to terms with it, is when they tell other people they are 'Bearing Up' implying that they are coping with the problem. A ship is also said to be bearing up after some catastrophe has happened - or is happening, and the difficult problem is under control.

Chock-a-Block When some people are completely fed up with something, or somebody - who might be most annoying - they may well say they are 'Chock-a-Block' or 'Chocker' with that situation or person. Such a saying means they can go no further, and comes from the nautical term of 'Chock-a-Block.' The meaning of this, is that when a tackle of blocks is in use, and those blocks are rove hard up to each other, the tackle is then said to be 'Chock-a-Block' - simply meaning that they can go no further.

Squaring up or **squared up** A well known term describing a vessel with its yards set at a 90 degree angle to the fore and aft line. The saying appears to have a number of meanings ie - A job has been completed - An area has been tidied up - Or even when a debt has been settled.

Clear the Yardarm Another saying which often has a business meaning, and one that has the same meaning as 'Squared Up' is one where a person has 'Cleared His Yardarm.' It may mean the orator of the phrase has settled a debt or disagreement.

By and Large Yet another phrase normally used by many people as an expletive. This term is now becoming increasingly common, and apparently means 'In general' or 'Generally speaking.' However, it is in reality nothing of the sort. In the days of the square riggers the term meant that when a ship was sailing with the wind before the beam, with its yards hauled around, that ship was 'By' the Wind. Then, if all plain sail is set, the ship was said to be sailing 'Large' The ship is therefore said to be sailing both 'By and Large.'

All Hands to the Pumps All hands to the pumps on a ship means the ship is filling with water, therefore, every single person on board is required to man the pumps in order to save the ship from sinking. The term has a similar meaning ashore when some emergency has arisen and all available personnel are required to help out.

Batten Down the Hatches Really means to cover up a ship's hatches, then secure them with battens and wedges to make the vessel watertight. The term when used by the landsman, usually indicates that all defensives are being used in an emergency.

There are also a number of nautical terms in everyday use which relate to boats

Shove Off This term comes from when a boat powered by oars may be alongside a ship or pier. An order from the coxswain to his bowman to 'Shove Off' has its obvious meanings, the bowman will use his oar to push the boat away from its berth. In everyday talk, a person being told to 'Push Off' or 'Shove Off' also has its meanings, it implies the person to whom the statement is made is to depart poste haste.

Pull Together Is yet another phrase coming from a boat's coxswain. The order means that the oarsmen must pull together and follow the 'Stroke Oar' whilst rowing. In our everyday talk, pulling together means virtually the same thing, it implies that a group of people should work as a team.

Pushing the Boat Out Another saying indicating that someone who is celebrating some activity or other is to spend big.

Missed the Boat People often talk of their having 'Missed the Boat' when some golden opportunity or other has passed them by. Sailors who have 'Missed The Boat' (The Liberty Boat) were the unlucky ones who were also out of luck by having had their leave stopped.

Sticking one's oar in When a boat's crew are at 'Oars' and one of the oarsmen dips his oar without an order from his coxswain, he is said to be 'Sticking His Oar In.' Similarly when a group of people are involved in some discussion and somebody interrupts, they may be said to be 'Sticking Their Oar In.'

Rocking the boat Anybody who is said to be 'Rocking The Boat' is of course causing a disturbance to normality. The same can be said if somebody stands up in a small boat and makes it roll dangerously.

Flogging a Dead Horse Another Phrase often heard is that of 'Flogging a Dead Horse.' This term also known as 'Working a Dead Horse' often arises, when it appears as though someone is working in vain or without reward. Its origins come from the days of sail, when a seaman had been given a one month advance wages after signing on his ship. Therefore, for the first month, and while working off his debt, he was said to be 'Working or Flogging a Dead Horse.'

Scuppered People talk of arrangements they've made that will fail; the plans then have to be 'Scuppered' The real term has no bearing on a ship's scuppers; it means defeat. Ships were often scuppered - or scuttled - to avoid being captured by their enemy.

Steady As She Goes Simply used to tell someone to keep things as they are. It is in fact an order to a ship's helmsman to maintain his new course.

At A Rate Of Knots This is a term used to describe something travelling at high speed, it is really an assessment of either a ship's or an aircraft's speed.

Swinging the Lead Here is another nautical term often spoken in a derogatory manner; it is used to describe someone who through his lazy attitude has shirked his responsibilities. 'Swinging the Lead' or better termed as 'Heaving the Lead' is however part of a sailor's duties, and one that is fully described in one of the chapters.

Fathom it Out Another common saying associated with heaving the lead is that of 'Fathom it Out.' This term often used in our everyday talk is usually made when someone is trying to solve some kind of a puzzle or intriguing question. In a puzzling situation someone may say they will 'Fathom It Out.' The ship's leadsman is in the same situation when he is trying to discover the depth of the seabed. He will therefore, 'Fathom Out' the seabed using his line which is marked off. Other of our everyday terms connected with heaving the lead are 'Taking A Sounding' or possibly 'Getting To the Bottom of Things' which also means a person is about to test, question, or discover something or other.

Laid Up A person is said to be 'Laid Up' when suffering from some accident or illness, the term may well arise from when a ship has been laid up through damage, or lack of a charter.

Hard Lines Often meaning some person or other has suffered some unexpected bad luck; just like a sailor who is up aloft in freezing conditions and has to work with frozen ropes, or 'Hard Lines.'

Taken on Board At times when one person makes a suggestion to another, and if approved of, his idea is said to be 'Taken on Board.'

Taking the Wind Out of One's Sails When one man threatens to take the wind out of another's sails, it generally means he is going to deflate him somewhat, or possibly stop him continuing in some activity. The term means the same in nautical jargon, and implies that the sails of a particular sailing vessel has had the wind blanketed from them thereby stopping the ship from making way.

Scandalise This term has nothing to do with gossip or unwanted publicity; it refers to a sail which has been temporarily shortened other than being reefed.

High and Dry People often say they've been left 'High and Dry' when they may have been deserted in time of need; just like a vessel which has been stranded on the beach or rocks.

Given a Wide Berth When some person or other is said to be given a 'Wide Berth' it generally means they're being avoided. Ships at sea are given a wide berth to lessen the possibility of collision.

Copper Bottomed A 'Copper Bottomed' agreement or contract is said to be one of high surety or integrity. The saying arises from when a wooden built ship is sheathed in copper and termed as being 'Copper Bottomed' or leak proof.

Blowing the Gaff A vessel which is 'Blowing its Gaff' has had its gaff sail blown out. It may also be said someone is 'Blowing his Gaff' when talking out of turn; although it isn't quite certain how the terms are related, the meaning is there.

Roped In A person is said to have been 'Roped In' when he has been trapped or commandeered for some unpleasant task.

Dressed To The Nines A person is said to be 'Dressed to the Nines' when he or she is looking most resplendent in some new or expensive attire. Apparently, the term comes from the Royal Navy, where a large number of different rigs of clothing are available for wear. When going ashore, or on parade, seamen at one time wore their best or number nine rig.

Sailing Too Close To The Wind When people are said to be 'Sailing Too Close To The Wind' it generally means they are living dangerously by taking chances. A ship of sail and especially a square rigger, also takes a huge chance when sailing close - or too close, to the wind. In the ships case, and when sailing close hauled, a sudden wind shift of just a few degrees from the wrong direction can easily send the sails aback and dismast the vessel.

Schooner Rigged This is a derogatory name given to someone who doesn't possess much in the way of clothing, and probably due to the unfortunate persons lack of finances. The term arises from ships of sail, when a vessel may have been reduced from a full rigger or barque to a schooner. As a matter of fact, this is just what happened to the *Cutty Sark* in 1916. When sailing under the Portuguese flag as the full rigged ship *Ferreira*, and after becoming dismasted, her owners couldn't afford the necessary repairs and had her 'Schooner Rigged' to save on costs.

Don't spoil the ship for a penn'orth O'Tar A general term in use when one person is being criticised for his parsimonious activities. The phrase originates from the days of sail, when wooden decks standing rigging and ship's sides were regularly tarred, and where missing out on one portion of the seaming may at a later date result in serious consequences for the ship.

Turning a Blind Eye A pretence of ignorance often displayed, when some order or other goes unheeded. This common saying arose ... when Horatio Nelson who was blind in one eye, was ordered by his flagship to disengage the action at the Battle of Copenhagen. Not agreeing with the order, he then raised his telescope to his blind eye towards the flagship to study the flag signal, then on declaring he couldn't see any such order, carried on fighting … and won the battle.

Stash away People often talk of stashing something away, and usually it is something illegal! The term comes from the days when opium merchants traded in China. Their cargoes of dope were said to be stashed or hidden away, and usually beneath other cargo. Then again, on the tea clippers a tea trader would wear a belt with a number of pockets in it. It was called a stash belt, and in each pocket was a differing brand of tea for examination by a prospective buyer.

To the Bitter End We often hear of someone who is going to fight on or continue to the bitter end. In fact, the Bitter End is the very last link of an anchor cable, the one that's shackled onto the ship in the cable locker.

Fore Sheets to the Wind

Some people use the term of being four sheets to the wind, three sheets to the wind and even two sheets to the wind. In reality, it is not a question of numbers, but of placement. The term 'Fore (not four) Sheets to the Wind' was in fact an order from the captain to slacken off the sheets of the foremast sails to allow those foremast sails to billow out on a following wind.

The Liverpool Yankee Clippers

In our modern times of space age technology, there are some types of yachts and multi-hulled sailing vessels that can travel through the water at a most astonishing speed. However, with regard to a days run of four hundred miles, it took these modern craft well over a century for them to catch up with their ancestors the clipper ships, and even today, those vessels are few and far between.

In the mid 19th century - the age of the ocean greyhounds - there were certain types or classes of clipper ships. These vessels were fast in comparison to the bluff bowed deep water men of previous times. However, there was one specific group of clipper ships that stood out from all the rest, and they were the 'Liverpool Yankee Clippers.'

The term 'Yankee Clipper' was a name derived from the vessels built in America for the Liverpool ship owner James Baines's Black Ball Line, and the White Star Line from the same port. The Americans who built these ships constructed them entirely of wood, and dozens of these magnificent sailing vessels were produced on the east coast of America. Those ships were successful because they were big and they were strong. Indeed, they were built for carrying large cargoes, a great number of passengers, and above all else 'speed.'

Amongst the many clippers that were built on either side of the Atlantic, there was one outstanding group that stood out from all the rest. This was 'The Four Hundred Club.' The requirements or credentials required for entry into that elitést group of ships, was the ability to sail 400 miles within 24 hours, and quite understandably the membership was small. As far as is known, and with the exception of the ***Marco Polo*** that was built at New Brunswick, and the Scottish built ***Lancing***, the only sailing ships ever to exceed 400 miles within 24 hours were all American built.

The Americans differed from the British in some of their measurements, and one of these was in ship tonnage. Their method of sail making was also different in the size of canvas cloths, as they normally had their sails made up from bolts 18 inches in width. After these bolts had been sewn together, with a double round seam of one and a half inches each side, the 'cloths' as they were termed, would be about 15 inches in width.

On the other hand, the British bolts of canvas were generally 24 inches for the larger sails, whilst 18 inch bolts were the norm for the smaller jibs or stay sails. Therefore, if and when the reef points were sewn into the centre of the cloth through a reef band, the American made sails had more reef points than the British did. The American made sails were also different in their appearancc. They were usually produced from heavy duck canvas or flax presenting a clean white image when caught in the sunlight. In comparison, the British canvas was a rather drab parchment colour; furthermore, it went even more colourless with aging or when stowed up on the yards for long periods. Therefore, American ships could often be identified by the whiteness of their sails and their narrowly set reef points.

Because of their enormous length and diameter, the lower wooden masts of all big ships like the Yankee Clippers were built with made masts. The term 'made masts' meant that because of their huge sizes, the ship's lower masts could hardly be fashioned from one tree alone. Therefore, in order to make up the huge diameter of the lower mast, which was normally about 42 inches in diameter, or 136 inches circumference, a large baulk of squared timber, or even two or three scarfed together, would be covered with a number of segments to make up the rounded circumference. At intervals of three feet, they would be banded together, or have iron hoops sweated onto them The practice of using 'made masts' went away with the advent of iron. However, some ships like **HMS *Victory*** and **USS *Constitution*** are two of the ships still afloat which have made masts.

James Baines Ship Owner

Born at Liverpool in 1823, James Baines was one of the most flamboyant characters ever to enter the list of Liverpool ship owners. Coming from a family of modest means, his father earned his living as a sugar refiner, whilst his mother who as a confectioner, sold her wares from their home in Upper Duke Street. Starting his working life as an apprentice engineer in the newly arrived world of steam, James Baines quickly departed from that employment, choosing instead to join his ship broking uncle Richard Baines in the world of maritime commerce. Uncle Richard employed his nephew as an apprentice shipping clerk, and indeed, it was from that lowly form of employment that the young James Baines developed. At the age of 23 in 1846 he bought a part share in the barque ***General Sale.*** Two years later, he married Jane Anne Browne a farmer's daughter from Netherton. No doubt she was a woman of some means, and probably the person who supplied the required finances to start him off in shipping.

Seeing the enormous opportunities of the day, which focused mainly on the Australian gold rush, Baines took a half share in the brig ***Vesta*** in 1851. The popular and persuasive ship owner then used his great charm to influence bankers and investors alike, and it wasn't long before a fleet of ships were beginning to form. At a later date, having bought the logo from an American firm for $1,000, The Black Ball Line of Liverpool was established. Under the command of the noted Bully Forbes, a recently acquired ship ***Marco Polo,*** was accredited with making a fantastic voyage to Australia. In this feat she was regarded as being the first ship ever, to sail over four hundred miles within 24 hours.

In 1852 Baines started the Black Ball Line, and in the short space of 14 years owned some of the greatest merchant sailing ships ever to sail under the red ensign. Baines was regarded as a spendthrift, and was indeed noted for his flamboyant and flash way of living. Whenever he wanted something it had to be the very best; therefore, when he wanted his ships built he went right to the top by having the finest. At the age of 29 he already had his horizons set, and upon realising no British yard could build for him the ships he wanted, an approach was made to the noted shipbuilder Donald McKay of Boston Massachusetts. McKay in turn produced four of the worlds fastest clipper ships for Baines; these four vessels which were specifically built for the Black Ball Line are described in the following chapters. As well as these four ships, five more second-hand McKay built vessels were bought in by the company which made nine McKay built ships in all.

Another Liverpool shipping concern was the White Star Line owned by John Pilkington and Henry Threlfall-Wilson. They were watching the activities of Baines closely, and not wanting to be overtaken also acquired the skilled services of the American ship builders. Therefore an approach was made to George Thomas of Rockland Maine - another of the leading east coast ship builders. He constructed for them the clippers ***White Star*** and ***Red Jacket***, both of which were designed by Samuel Pook. These two vessels were to prove the equal of the Black Ballers. The ships of the Black Ball and White Star Lines were then to become known worldwide as 'The Liverpool Yankee Clippers.'

In the growing commercial world of 1855 the Post Office wanted a faster mail link with Australia, and the contract was something that James Baines dearly wanted. However, there was fierce competition for it - and especially from London. In order to beat off any rivalry and ensure he had the largest slice of the cake, the wily Baines approached the White Star Line, which was of course, one of his competitors. Between the two companies who had the biggest and fastest ships in Britain, they formed a monopoly.

To frighten off any rivalry, Baines even gave a guarantee to the Post Office of a 65 day land to land delivery service. The shipping critics of the day were astounded at such a claim, they wouldn't accept that any ship could ever reach Australia in such a short period of time. However, after accepting a penalty clause of £100 a day on anything over 65 days, the result was that the monopolistic contract was awarded to the two Liverpool ship owners. At last, the Black Ball and White Star Lines were able to operate an organised mail service to Australia. The mail contract sole rights for the service were now controlled from Liverpool and not London. However, with regard to the penalty clause of £100 a day accepted by Baines, it was to cost him dearly in the end.

James Baines spent money like there was no tomorrow, his ships were lavishly fitted out, and he himself lived in great style. He hosted numerous parties, and was most generous to his employees. Indeed, it was possibly his extravagant way of life that contributed to his downfall. The firm continued to grow, and at one point in the history of the Black Ball Line, there were 134 ships in its service; a figure that included a large number of ships on charter.

With the end of the Australian gold rush, it was also the end of the Black Ball Line, because with a lack of Aussie gold diggers, there was also the added absence of the huge numbers of passengers that used to fill the ships. More importantly though, was the £100 a day penalty clause, and all these facts added up to the ruin of James Baines. Indeed, the critics were right, for a 65 day passage was seldom completed. The Black Ball Line started going into decline, and by 1866 Baines was bankrupt.

His creditors wanted their money back, therefore, his fleet had to be sold off. He wasn't without friends though, Thomas Harrison another Liverpool ship owner bought some of his ships then leased them back to him. Although James Baines made another attempt at resurrecting his Black Ball Line, the company never recovered, and in 1871 he once again went bankrupt. Nevertheless, and despite his folly, James Baines will always be remembered as one of Liverpool's greatest ship owners. Idling out his last years whilst lodging at the home of one of his friends. James Baines died with cirrhosis of the liver at the age of 66.

Some writers and researchers appear to be confused with the names of Thomas Harrison and Thomas & James Harrison ... as well as the Black Ball Line ship *Lightning* and other of the company vessels. According to Captain Graeme Cubbin, who at the time of writing is the chairman of the Liverpool Nautical Research Society, and also the curator of T&J Harrison's company museum, there were at least three Liverpool ship owners bearing the name of Thomas Harrison. There were also ship owners similarly named from London, Glasgow and Whitby. However, Thomas & James Harrison of Liverpool, later to be known as The Charente Steamship Company, never at any time bought or chartered any of the Black Ball Line's ships.

James Baines who lived from 1823 until 1889. He was regarded as the most flamboyant and entrepreneurial of all Liverpool's ship owners.

Donald McKay the noted shipbuilder from Boston Massachusetts. He built four of the worlds finest clipper ships for the Liverpool Black Ball Line.

Marco Polo

One of the most famous and noted of all clipper ships, and one of the few that has sailed through the 400 miles in a day barrier, was the much celebrated full rigged ship ***Marco Polo***. Completed in 1850, she was built and owned by James Smith of Marsh Creek, New Brunswick. The ***Marco Polo*** being built entirely of wood, had the contemporary 'made' masts with single topsails, single t'gallants and royals. With a tonnage was 1,625 in the new measurement, she had a length of 184.1 and a beam of 36.3 feet.
James Smith had originally built the ***Marco Polo*** as a timber carrier, and during her construction timber ports had been built into the ship's bows. These ports were common place in timber carriers, and so constructed for the huge baulks that couldn't be loaded through the hatchways. The ship was noted for her being built box like, in fact there was no difference at all in the height between foc'sle head and poop deck. Indeed, she has been quoted in being built as 'square as a brick.' The ***Marco*** had a short sharp entrance - as the model picture shows - with a rather longer departure. Her depth was about five feet more than a similar ship of her size, and it was this extra draught that apparently gave her the great stability she was noted for.
The ***Marco*** had a broad square stern, and this was decorated with the head of an elephant at the centre, then there was a carved figure of Marco Polo on both sides of that centre piece. On the squash bows there was the full length figurehead of Marco Polo himself. The ship's side was black, on which there were thirteen painted gun ports over a broad white band; the masts and jib-boom were buff with the bowsprit and yards black
The maiden voyage of the ***Marco Polo*** began from St Johns on 1 June 1851, in her hold she had a full cargo of timber that was delivered to Liverpool on June 19. She then sailed to Mobile where a cargo of cotton was returned for the mills of Lancashire; this passage took 35 days. While she was in Liverpool the ship was put up for sale, but because of her box like appearance, little interest was shown in her by any of the ever alert ship owners. However, James Baines who'd recently joined the Liverpool Ship Owners Association took a fancy to her robust appearance, and within a short space of time had purchased the vessel for £9,000. At that particular time the Australian immigrant trade was booming, and Baines immediately had the vessel converted into a packet ship.
The ***Marco Polo*** was the Black Ball Line's first ship, and on her first voyage under the company house flag, she netted a huge sum of £13,000, a figure that was more than her purchase and conversion costs. During that 1852 voyage she was commanded by Bully Forbes, a man who didn't take kindly to anybody who opposed him in the slightest. The

ship which had a crew of 59 took 930 immigrants out to Melbourne. Unfortunately, there were 52 deaths during the outward passage, but during the same trip nine births were recorded.

The record for a passage between the UK and Melbourne had been 76 days dock to dock; this was made by the ***Constance*** in 1850. However, in his efforts to emulate that passage, Bully Forbes drove his ship for all she was worth. It has been mythically said, that he put padlocks on the sheets then stood over them with a loaded revolver … as had Bully Waterman! With more than her fair share of wind and weather, the ***Marco Polo*** absolutely tore through the Southern Ocean, and by the time she sighted Cape Otway, she was just 68 days land to land - and had beaten **Constance's** record by eight days - a new record!

Desertions by sailors were commonplace in Australia, and quite often a captain would have to pay a large amount of money for replacements. However, Captain James Nicol Forbes had formulated a plan to discourage such happenings. As soon as the ship arrived in Melbourne, Bully Forbes had the whole crew arrested and locked up ashore. Then after the ship had been discharged, loaded, and ready to sail, he had them all returned. The ***Marco Polo*** arrived back in the River Mersey on Boxing Day 1852, this was another record passage. The whole voyage that started at Liverpool on 4 July 1852, ended at the same port on 26 December 1852. Five months and twenty two days … another record!

Marco Polo **in the River Mersey from a painting by Thomas Dove. Note the absolutely flat deck which was the fashion of the times. She is also flying the White ensign from aft and a Union Jack from forrard.** ***Liverpool County Museums***

Lightning

In the 19th century there appears to have been a number of vessels bearing the name, ***Lightning.*** However, none of them should be confused with the one that was built by Donald McKay, because this vessel was to go down in maritime history. The ***Lightning*** was the first of the four extreme clippers to be built for the Liverpool Black Ball Line. Indeed, it was on her maiden passage from Boston to Liverpool on 1 March 1854, that she logged 436 nautical miles; a record that will stand for all time for a British full rigged ship.

Another of her distinctions was she was the first ship ever, to be built in America for service under the red ensign. Furthermore, at that particular time she was the largest ship in the British merchant service. The ***Lightning*** was 2,083 US tons on completion, a huge ship with nothing of her size ever having been seen in the British Mercantile Marine. The length of the ship on deck was 237 feet, and between its perpendiculars 243 feet, added to which, was a further 90 feet for the bowsprit, jib boom and stern overhang; her maximum length therefore, was some 333 feet.

On completion the ship had royals, then at a later date she crossed sky sails on all three masts, the main-mast truck was 164 feet above the deck, and when light ship she towered almost 200 feet above the Mersey waters. The fore, and mizzen masts were 151 and 115 feet respectively. In all she could set 13,000 running yards of canvas, and all this was before the mast-heads were raised to allow for moon sails. The ship's beam measurement was 44 feet and she had a depth of hold of 23 feet.

Lightning's first captain was the noted James Nicol Forbes - otherwise known as Bully Forbes. He'd come from ***Marco Polo*** after having made a great reputation, and it is to him - as well as the ***Lightning***, - that the record run of 436 miles belongs. When the ***Lightning*** left Boston, there was still some work left to be finished off in Liverpool. This included the furnishings of the passenger accommodation as well as the coppering of the underwater hull. These items added a further £2,000 to her building cost of £30,000. The work could be done at a much cheaper price in Liverpool, and it set the pattern for the rest of the ships that were built in America for the Black Ball Line.

Lightning's maiden voyage began from Liverpool on 14 May 1854, and to accompany him on the trip, Bully Forbes had the equally noted hard case Bully Brag as his first mate.

The *Lightning* of the Liverpool Black Ball Line, holds the all time speed record for a full rigged ship. On 1 March 1854, under the command of James Nicol Forbes, she logged 436 nautical miles. Black Ball Line ships could always be identified by the black ball sewn into their fore topsails.

Authors Collection

The voyage to Australia was a great success and the 'Yankee Clipper' arrived back in the Mersey after a voyage that had lasted just 5 months and 9 days.
After he'd completed another successful round voyagc from Liverpool to Melbourne, Captain Forbes was relieved by Captain Anthony Enright. The new captain knew all about fast ships, in fact his last was the noted tea clipper ***Chrisolite***.
On completion of his first trip in the ship, a number of alterations were made with the main deck being covered in to make it an upper 'tween deck. This was then a complete deck from the poop to the forecastle. On Captain Enright's further recommendations, a false bow was fitted resulting in the hollow concave flares of the bows being filled in. This was a practice that had been highly successful on some ships, and indeed, increased the speed of those vessels. However in the case of the ***Lightning*** it was a huge mistake. The ship had been so well designed and built in the first place, that any extra speed was not possible.
During the course of ***Lightning's*** next passage to Melbourne, the timbers that were used in the construction of the false bow worked loose. They came adrift to such an extent, that the dragging effect of those timbers - which due to the weather, could not be discarded at sea - this resulted in the ship taking an extra week to make her destination.
Lightning made seven more round trips between Liverpool and Melbourne before being chartered by the British government. In this new role she went around from Liverpool to Portsmouth; from there 650 troops were transported to Calcutta as part of a force to deal with the Indian Mutiny. She then resumed as a passenger ship and was most popular with both passengers and crew alike. ***Lightning*** carried a full compliment of around 85, and of these 48 were sailors. Many of this crew had been in the vessel since new and knew no other ship.
In all her career excepting the one odd trip to India ***Lightning*** had never been more than 84 days between ports. She was regular, the food and conditions were good, and whereas most ships visiting Australia suffered large scale crew desertions, it was one thing on the ***Lightning*** which seldom took place. At the Black Ball Line offices in Liverpool, there was a proverbial queue a mile long waiting for a berth in any of their ships.

The end of the Lightning

The end of the *Lightning* occurred on 31 October 1869. This was whilst she was at Geelong almost loaded and ready to sail for Liverpool. But it was on that fateful day that smoke and fire was discovered coming from the hold. The ship was built entirely of wood, and even though every effort was made to put the fire out, it soon took hold and began to blaze. It was then realised that because the water in the dock was too shallow, the ship could not be scuttled to be raised at a later date. The ***Lightning*** was eventually towed out into the river and eventually scuttled. But alas, it was too late to save the famous ship, the fire intensified and her foremast came down in the blazing inferno. Although much of the cargo was later salved, the ***Lightning*** became a total loss. The shipping fraternity were shocked at the loss of such an already world famous ship.

Champion of the Seas

The second of the Liverpool Yankee Clippers to come from Donald McKay's yard was the ***Champion Of The Seas.*** Launched just three months after the ***Lightning***, this new acquisition to the Black Ball Line took the mantle from her predecessor, by becoming Britain's largest merchant ship. The 2,447 US ton ***Champion Of The Seas*** had also been built at East Boston and was launched in April 1854. Whereas in a ship's gross tonnage the American tons are slightly smaller than the Imperial tons, she was later certified in the UK at 1,947 GRT. In being a little larger all around than the ***Lightning,*** her length between perpendiculars was 252 feet, this resulted in the overall measurements from the tip of her jib boom to the taffrail being 337 feet, her beam was 45 feet 6 inches and depth of hold just over 23 feet.

Her first Commander was Captain Alexander Newlands, a master of note who had also superintended her construction. On completion the new ship was towed around from Boston, and after having loaded her first cargo at New York, she sailed for Liverpool in June 1854. Although she took a disappointing 16 days to make the crossing, a time any other ship would have been proud of - her so-called long passage was due to lack of wind. Nevertheless, she still proved to be a fast ship when the wind did come up. However, she apparently never had the speed of ***Lightning*** as her underwater lines were not as sharp. Like all the Black Ballers the ship was well built with no expense spared; on deck, her 'made' lower masts, which were 42 inches in diameter, were supported by eleven and a half inch four stranded shrouds, made from the finest Russian hemp. On the ship's arrival at Liverpool, just like the ***Lightning***, she had her bottom coppered in the Canning Dock before being fitted out internally as a packet ship. For a figure head she had a sailor wearing a navy tunic with bell bottomed trousers, whilst her stern was adorned with the Australian coat of arms.

During the course of her maiden voyage to Melbourne, it was claimed that the ***Champion Of The Seas*** sailed 465 sea miles in 24 hours. Although it will never be known if she ever did accomplish that feat, the claim was later discounted by the critics and experts of the day, as the claimed distance was based on dead reckoning. After doing the Liverpool to Melbourne run, the 'Champ' was also chartered by the British government to ferry troops to Calcutta, The general idea being, that because the ships of the Black Ball Line had built up such a reputation of well being, speed and reliability, they could transport the troops out to India faster than any other ships could. On 3 August 1857, ***Champion Of The Seas*** left Portsmouth with 1,000 troops as well as a crew of over 100. However, the speedy delivery of the soldiers was not to be, for the ships making the passage were held up by lack of wind in the Bay of Bengal. Eventually, the ***Champion Of The Seas*** took 103 days to make the Sandheads at the mouth of the River Hoogley, a passage she was expected and hoped to make in 70 days or even less. When the charter was over, she resumed her Liverpool - Melbourne service until the year 1866.

By that time James Baines her owner had gone into severe financial difficulties. In order to pay off some of his creditors, the ***Champion Of The Seas*** was reluctantly sold for £9,750, to his close friend and confidant Thomas Harrison. Apparently, Thomas Harrison only made the purchase with the purpose of helping his friend out, and on acquiring the ship immediately leased it back to him. Due to the gold rush being over and fierce competition from all sides, the fast moving days of the Australian passenger trade were getting thin, and soon afterwards, the ***Champion Of The Seas*** went tramping for anything on offer. In 1873, after having run onto a sand bank and being badly hogged she struggled back to Liverpool. It was then discovered that her softwood timbers were also showing signs of rot, as well as having become badly strained in her stranding. With these repairs in mind she was sold for £7,500. Although her damaged timbers were repaired, the problem of leaks persisted and her pumps were often manned for long periods.

In order to survive the harsh realities of maritime business, the 'Yankee Clipper' which had once been amongst the proudest in the Mersey, had since been reduced to taking low class freights. Her last voyage found her at Callao, where after having been loaded with guano bird droppings, the strained, waterlogged and leaking ship set sail for Cork. She left the Peruvian port in January 1877.

However, in quite moderate weather whilst off Cape Horn she began taking water. Her pumps that were apparently choked with the guano couldn't be worked. At that particular time and most fortunately for those on board, the weather was good and her distress signals were seen by the barque ***Windsor.*** This vessel stood by in the hope that the ***Champion of the Seas*** could be saved. Unfortunately, when the water rose higher and all hope of saving the ship had gone, her crew were forced to abandon ship. They were then taken on board the ***Windsor*** as the ***Champion of the Seas*** slowly filled and eventually foundered on 31 January 1877.

James Baines

The ship ***James Baines*** was of course named after her owner, and when she was launched in July 1854, she became the third of the quartet of the Black Ball Line's Yankee Clippers. Larger than the previous two, her measurements were 266 x 44.75 x 24 feet; her UK gross tonnage was 2,275. On her delivery passage from Boston to Liverpool, and under the command of Captain Charles McDonnell, she created a new Atlantic crossing record by making the trip in 12 days 6 hours to the Mersey Rock Light. Although she never had the winds for long during her passage, she did manage to make an average 20 knots during one watch, with a best day's run of 337 miles between her noon day sightings.

The imminent arrival of Liverpool's newest ship was signalled from Bidston Hill, and from there, further messages were relayed that sent a rapid message to her owners in Liverpool. Word spread fast, and by the time ***James Baines*** arrived in the Mersey in September 1854, huge crowds had gathered to see her at the waterfront, and what a sight she must have made with her impressive length and towering masts.

In Liverpool she was coppered, fitted out and as usual had every conceivable extra added. The figurehead was an effigy of James Baines himself, complete with top hat, coat and tails. Having been made in Liverpool, the figurehead had been shipped over to Boston for the launch. The ship's stern was adorned with the coat of arms of both England and America.

The accommodation and rig of the ship was in keeping with the other Yankee Clippers. The main yard was 100 feet long, and on her mainmast she carried a skysail with the facilities for a moon sail. In all, ***James Baines*** carried over 13,000 running yards of canvas, from 18 inch bolts, this figure did not include the stun sails or other kites.

Her maiden voyage began from Liverpool on 9 December 1854, and on that passage she took 700 passengers to Melbourne in 65 days. During the passage, she twice broke through the barrier of 400 miles in twenty-three and a half hours. On her homeward run which began on 12 March 1855, she once again went through the 400 mile mark, arriving in the Mersey after a 69 day passage. On her second voyage which started in April 1856, and due to many windless days and mild seas, a slow passage was experienced both out and home. The whole trip took 7 months and 12 days - 2 months more than expected or planned for. However, she did once again go through the 400 miles barrier when outward bound. Her third voyage was unfortunately to be her last to the colonies. On the outward run she was beaten five days by her stable companion ***Lightning,*** but on the homeward run, ***James Baines*** beat the ***Lightning*** by six days. Both these ships as well as ***Champion Of The Seas*** were then chartered by the government to transport troops to India. When the ships were at Portsmouth they were paid a visit by Queen Victoria, who after walking through the vessels on a formal inspection, made the most complimentary remarks about their condition and also the well being of the Mercantile Marine. ***James Baines*** left Portsmouth on 8 August 1857, she had a full passenger quota, but instead of her normal passengers, this time it was 1,000 soldiers from the 97th Regiment. Like the rest of the large fleet that had a similar contingent of troops, she was held up by lack of good winds ... and especially in the Bay of Bengal. Eventually, she made the Sandheads after 101 days. At Calcutta, the troops were disembarked to quell the Indian Mutiny. A full cargo of jute, rice, linseed and hides were then loaded for her home port of Liverpool. The ship had only a small number of passengers for the homeward run, and the voyage ended at Liverpool on 16 April 1858.

To discharge her cargo, the ***James Baines*** was berthed in the Huskisson Dock amongst the Cunard and the White Star Line's transatlantic packets. Discharging of her cargo then began, but alas! when the after 'tween deck had been cleared on April 22, smoke was to be seen coming up from the lower hold of the main hatch. When the 'tween deck hatch boards were removed to tackle the impending fire, the fresh air fed the flames and started an inferno. The result being that the blaze was soon out of control. In an attempt to save the ship, she was scuttled alongside at her berth, but the water around the ship was too shallow to sink her. Soon afterwards the masts went over the side in the blaze, and despite an heroic fight by the primitive and poorly equipped fire brigade, she burnt to the water line.

Ships in the close proximity of the fire then had been moved away to save them from the same fate. After the fire had finally been extinguished, the ***James Baines*** was declared a total loss but much of her cargo was later salved. According to the writings of Basil Lubbock, what was left of her wooden hull and frames were used in the construction of the Liverpool Landing Stage. The one distinction the ***James Baines*** holds, is she sailed through the 400 miles a day barrier more times than any other ship.

The Yankee Clipper *James Baines*. She sailed through the four hundred miles a day barrier more times than any other ship.

Authors Collection

Model of the ship James Baines

Donald McKay

Launched at Donald McKay's Boston yard in January 1855, this ship was the last of the famous quartet of Black Ball Line clippers. Not quite as sharp as the ***Lightning*** or ***James Baines*** - except that she was a little larger all round, ***Donald McKay*** greatly resembled the ***Champion Of the Seas.*** Furthermore, another one of James Baines's ships had the distinction of being Britain's largest merchant ship. It also emphasised the fact that in being brilliant as he was, her builder Donald McKay was most inconsistent in his ship designing.

The *Donald McKay* came off the ways in January 1855 and was 2,614 tons. She had a length of 266 feet, a beam 46 feet 3 inches, and a depth of 29 feet 5 inches. The masts and their heights were in keeping with the other Yankee Clippers, although with a larger sail plan she could set 17,000 running yards of canvas.

Mr Baines the owner named the ship after the builder as a tribute to his contribution to the industry, as well as the fact that the two men had built up an excellent working relationship. Mr Donald McKay was a Canadian, although as his name implies he was of Scots descent, and to mark this, the ship's figure head was of a Scottish highlander dressed in the tartan of the McKay Clan.

Sailing on her delivery passage from Boston to Liverpool on 21 February 1855, the ***Donald McKay*** was under the command of Captain Warner. Mr McKay also went to the UK on the passage, and he said he was well satisfied with the ship's performance. Although by clipper standards the ship had a slow passage of 17 days, she did prove that by logging 421 miles in a strong gale on February 27, she was indeed an ocean thorough-bred if given the wind.

The ship was enormous, she had three decks and her passenger accommodation consisted of 36 staterooms with the rest of the living spaces being beautifully furnished. In all she could carry over 1,000 passengers with a crew of around 120.

Like the other Yankee Clippers of the Black Ball Line, the ***Donald McKay*** went on the profitable and busy Australian run. Missing out on the trip to India in 1857, she stayed on the run for 13 years until 1868 when with ***Champion Of The Seas,*** she went under the ownership of Thomas Harrison of Liverpool. The ***Donald McKay*** was then leased back to

Mr Baines who continued to operate her in what was a dwindling trade, and one where the end of the once magnificent Black Ball Line was much in sight. In 1874, the ***Donald McKay*** was the subject of an auction in London which realised £8,750, the new owner was JS De Wolfe of Liverpool. The ship was then used as a troopship ferrying 1,000 of the Connaught Rangers out to Bombay; for her new owner it was a most profitable voyage, because on the return passage to the UK under Captain Richards, a further 1,000 soldiers were shipped home.

JS De Wolfe kept the ship for five years using her as a general cargo carrier, but in 1879, ***Donald McKay*** the last of the famous four, was sold to a German owner. Retaining her much vaunted name she continued her career in trading between Bremen and New York, until eventually, the ***Donald McKay*** - the largest clipper ship ever built to sail under the red ensign - was sold for use as a coal hulk at Madeira. She didn't last long in her new employment, for after having caught fire at her moorings and not being considered worthy of the repair estimate, she was broken up in 1890.

It remains, that of the four Liverpool Yankee Clippers built for the Black Ball Line, all of them ended their careers in tragic circumstances. Three of them were burned in port whilst the other one foundered off Cape Horn.

Schomberg

The clipper ship ***Schomberg*** was quick to gain prominence in the shipping world. However, it was not her sailing records or fast passages that made the headlines. It was because like so many other ships past and present, she was lost on her maiden voyage. Launched at Aberdeen on 5 April 1855, she came from the yard of Alexander Hall and was christened by Mr James Layard MP. The ship was named after Captain Schomberg RN, who was the chief immigration officer at the port of Liverpool at that particular time. Great things were expected of the ship when she arrived in the Mersey on July 11. Her captain was the noted James Nicol Forbes of ***Marco Polo*** and ***Lightning*** fame, and he'd brought the ship around from her Dundee builders to Liverpool in ten days.

With his high ranking as a sailing master, it would appear that Bully Forbes had been specially selected for the task of commanding the ***Schomberg,*** and probably to further enhance the fast growing name of The Black Ball Line. The latest addition to the James Baines fleet was indeed a big ship; her registered tonnage was 2,400, whilst her other dimensions were 288 x 45 x 29.2. She was by far the largest clipper ship ever to be built in Britain.

Six months after her launch on 6 October 1855, the ***Schomberg*** sailed from Liverpool for Melbourne. She carried 430 passengers in well found accommodation, whilst in her hold, there was over 3,000 tons of cargo consisting mainly of track lines for the Geelong Railway. The ***Schomberg*** never had the desired winds during the passage, and the first sighting of the Australian coast after an 80 day passage, was that of Cape Bridgewater at 1 pm on Christmas Day 1855. The ship was stood off the land with the wind blowing fresh from ESE, then at 6 pm on Wednesday the 27th with the wind coming from the same direction, the ship was four miles off land and Captain Forbes stood in again. But at 11 pm when an attempt was made to tack away from the land the helm refused to answer, this resulted in the captain having to wear ship.

Unfortunately, there was an unchartered three knot current running westward which carried the ship onto a sand spit. The grounding occurred about 35 miles west of Cape Otway. At the time of the ship stranding, the master went below and left Mr Keene the mate in charge. Given the gravity of the situation this was most unusual and brought even further resentment from the passengers towards the captain who hadn't been at all popular during the passage.

Suddenly the ship was in grave danger, all sail was taken in, boats were lowered to land

Schomberg

After being launched on 5 April 1855, the *Schomberg* is seen in the above photograph being rigged out at her builder's yard in Aberdeen. Her lower masts were so large in diameter, that she was fitted with 'made masts.' This term of made masts is described in the glossary. Note the white painted iron bands that encircle the lower masts; these are for holding the mast segments together. Note also the ship's outside channels that supported the twelve inch diameter natural fibre lower shrouds. A canvas on both bow and stern covers some activity such as the new scroll work being painted in the rain. The *Schomberg* was the largest ever of the clipper ship breed to be built in Britain.
This was the ship that went aground and was lost on her maiden voyage, thus damaging irreparably the reputation of Bully Forbes.

the passengers, guns were then fired and rockets set off. These signals of distress attracted the steamer ***Queen,*** which under the command of Captain Doran was bound for Portland. He took all the passengers off, then after turning back on his course landed them all safely at Melbourne, but the ***Schomberg*** soon became a total loss.

A court of inquiry was later held at Melbourne into the stranding of the ship, and charges were brought against Captain Forbes and the third mate Mr Saxby. The master was tried on a number charges, one of which, was his failure to order the anchors away. The bosun also gave evidence against Captain Forbes, although it later transpired that he had been bribed by some of the passengers to give false evidence. So unpopular was Bully Forbes

The life of Jane Forbes may well be considered to have been short at 33. But that of Bully Forbes at the age of 52, was the norm for those who lived in the nineteenth century.

Photo By Mark Wong

with the passengers, that the bosun had apparently been promised a government post if the charges against the master could be sustained. However, the bosun failed to appear in court on the second day of the inquiry, the court became suspicious, and this resulted in his evidence being ruled out. Although Captain Forbes was committed for trial, he was acquitted on the grounds of the unchartered three knot current which had sent his ship ashore. On his return to Liverpool, Captain Forbes was given command of the ***Hastings*** another of the Black Ball Line ships. He wandered around for a while until 1857, before being given command of the very ship which first made him a name - the ***Marco Polo***. Captain Forbes died at the age of 52 and was buried at Liverpool's Smithdown Road cemetery.

Criffel

A story given to the author by Captain Joseph Kay, the grandson of Captain Thomas Kay.

The three masted barque ***Criffel*** was built for the small but highly respected firm of McDiarmid and Company. This was one of a number of shipping companies that had their offices at 16 Water Street Liverpool.
Coming from the Maryport yard of Ritsons, ***Criffel*** registered 1,249 gross and 1,195 nett tons. At the time of her being built in 1891, Captain SA Buley was quoted as saying 'Due to slack times, the vessel was constructed mainly by the apprentice shipbuilders of Ritsons, and although the ***Criffel*** may not have been the prettiest of ships, she was most certainly well built.'
After having left school in Falmouth, young Buley began his sea career at the age of 14 and then joined his first ship the brigantine ***Gem*** in 1896. After having learned the rudiments of sail, he later passed through the ranks of ordinary seaman to able seaman, then eight years after joining his first ship, he signed on the ***Criffel*** as its first mate. Although a 22 year old mate on a deep sea ship was considered to be extremely young, it must be borne in mind that most of his counterparts had opted for the comparatively easier life of steamships; nevertheless, even at that tender age he was a man of quite some experience.
Buley joined the ***Criffel*** at Bristol in 1904, his master Captain A Billet had been in the ship since new. Under Captain Billet's command the ***Criffel*** had at times experienced some close shaves, the most serious of which was when a hold fire broke out whilst the vessel was in New York. At the time she was loaded with case oil and 250 tons of explosives. Amidst the great pandemonium where people rushed for their lives, the blaze was extinguished by the fire brigade; they used fire floats and scuttled the ship alongside.
From then on the ***Criffel*** hardly came to notice, until the year 1906 when she was leaving Sydney bound for Newcastle NSW. At that time and during the hours of darkness, ***Criffel*** was under the charge of the France Fenwick tug ***Advance.*** Whilst under tow, she had a smaller vessel ***Morora*** secured alongside her. Due to the length of the tow line, which was probably the deep sea length of 100 fathoms, the Howard Smith passenger steamer ***Buningyong*** which was going full ahead, erroneously crossed between the tow.
The outcome was that ***Criffel's*** bowsprit sliced right through the upper works of the ***Buningyong,*** and this resulted in the whole of the steamer's superstructure being ripped

off. Miraculously, and although there were 129 passengers as well as the crew on the steamer, there were no casualties on board.
However, the collision caused the engine room of the steamer to flood. The tug immediately dropped her tow and secured a line onto the stricken vessel before beaching her in the safety of Rushcutter Bay.
As a testimony to her being so well built by a group of apprentices, the only damage to ***Criffel,*** was a fractured bowsprit and a twisted stem. She was then referred to as 'The Sydney Battleship' by the locals. Captain Billet who'd been in the vessel for 15 years had always taken a pride in his ship and crew, and indeed many of his own officers had served their apprenticeship on the ***Criffel*** with him. One of them was later to become the marine superintendent of the Cunard White Star Line, whilst yet another, became the chief officer of the Cunard White Star Liner ***Queen Mary.***
The ***Criffel*** was due to sail before the inquiry into the collision could be held, and due to these circumstances Captain Billet was required to attend the hearing. In the absence of its master therefore, the first mate would normally take command of the ship. However, representatives of the company in Sydney considered the 23 year Buley too young for the post. As no replacements were readily available, an approach was made to Captain Thomas Kay formerly of the ***Falls Of Garry*** to command the ***Criffel.***
Although Captain Kay had retired from the sea and was married in Sydney; he like so many other genuine seamen couldn't resist the temptation to come out of retirement. Due to the length of the hearing, Captain Billet stayed in Sydney for several months; eventually coming home as a passenger on one of the P&O Line ships.
On 3 August 1906, the three masted barque sailed for Mollendo with coal, but after having discharged her cargo Buley suffered an injury. The accident occurred whilst he was supervising the stowage of the kedge anchor, this left him with a crushed hand resulting in him having to be paid off. He came home to Liverpool minus a finger on the PSNC ship SS ***Orita.*** From the West Coast the ***Criffel*** returned to Sydney to load a cargo of grain for the UK, eventually arriving at Barry in August 1907. Captain Kay who'd then been at sea for 44 years paid off and retired for the second time. The previously injured mate SA Buley had been kept on half pay whilst convalescing, and this was considered an act of great generosity by the firm. Better still was yet to come, for on Captain Kay's departure back to Sydney, Buley was given his first command at the age of 24.
At first the owners suggested an older and more experienced first mate should be assigned to the vessel; however, to avoid any possible intimidation, the new Captain Buley decided on someone younger than himself for the position. Eventually, a Mr Pennant aged 22 was signed on as first mate, with the second mate being Mr Flemming who was aged 19.

Built in 1902 the *Colonial Empire* **was a 2,436 ton four masted barque. In 1910 she was sold to Cook & Dundas who kept her until she was wrecked.**
As seen below in this 1917 photo, she is hard and fast on Thunderbolt Reef, Algoa Bay. She was later declared a total loss. ***Photos - Captain John Kay***

Leaving Newport with coal for Montevideo, the ***Criffel*** was taken as far as Lundy Island under tow. Leaving on the same tide and also bound for Montevideo was the much bigger ***Colonial Empire***. On arriving at the mouth of the River Plate, the ***Criffel*** was bombarded by a huge swarm of locusts, then on the same night she was hit by a Pampero. Eventually, after a 70 day passage the ***Criffel*** arrived at Montevideo - but ***Colonial Empire*** had been there for ten days! After having discharged early in 1908, the ***Criffel*** was ordered out to Adelaide in ballast. The ***Colonial Empire*** which had taken the same charter had sailed four days earlier.

Criffel sailed extremely well in ballast, and for Captain Buley the race with the big barque was on. He was determined to at least make up some of the four days the ***Colonial Empire*** had on him, and by which token he could declare himself the winner. The passage around the Horn and across the Pacific was good, and indeed, every minute of every day was raced.

When the ***Criffel*** was in sight of Kangaroo Island 52 days later, a four masted barque hove into view. It was the ***Colonial Empire!*** Captain Buley had won his first race. At Newcastle, Captain Simpson of the ***Colonial Empire*** congratulated his younger opposite number, and from then on the two became the best of friends.

From Newcastle both ships were ordered to different ports of the WCSA with coal, then

The *Criffel* was Captain Buley's first command, it was also Captain Thomas Kay's last.

From a painting of John Kay

back to the Australian coast in ballast. At Melbourne the two ships met up once again, and from which port they took the same charter of grain for the UK. At a later date another remarkable coincidence occurred when both ships arrived at Falmouth for orders on the same day. Captain Buley and Captain Simpson had lunch together before the ***Colonial Empire*** proceeded to Hamburg with her cargo.

After two years of sailing almost alongside each other, Captain Buley in his memoirs wrote that Captain Simpson was the best friend he'd ever had in all his time on ships; but after the meeting at Falmouth they never met again. The ***Criffel*** went on to Plymouth where it was learned she'd been sold to the Norwegians.

It was Captain Buley's first and last command under sail; from then on he was unable to maintain his captain's position as sailing vessels were becoming scarcer by the day. Most fortunately for him however, Mr McDiarmid introduced him to the manager of Lowden & Co, a firm who also had their offices at 16 Water Street. Due to this meeting and thanks to Mr McDiarmid, he was given the post of first mate on one of Lowden's ships the SS ***Baroda.*** Then within a year he was once again given a command, this time in the SS ***Manx Isles,*** a vessel in which he served throughout the First World War. In 1919, and after having served 23 years at sea, the 37 year old Captain Buley retired to a shore job .

The Ships on which Thomas Kay served during his forty four years sea service

Ship	Registered At	GRT	Rig	Rank	Dates of Service	Length of service	Owners
Martha	St. Johns N.B.	1,032	Ship	O.S.	03-08-1863 - 03-08-1863	4M 4D	Gilberg & Co.
Supberb	Liverpool			O.S.	11-08-1863 - 16-05- 1865	1Y 9M 5D	
Undine	Liverpool			O.S.	18-08-1865 - 19-12-1865	2m 1D	
Prioress	Liverpool			A.B.	15-08-1865 - 19-12-1865	4M 4D	
Nova Scotian	Gaysboro N.S.	284		A.B.	22-01-1866 - 06-07-1866	5M 14D	O & H.Davies
Virginia	Windsor N.S.	934		A.B.	23-07-1866 - 15-11-1866	3M 23D	G Armstrong
Cleta	London	546	Composite Barque	A.B.	28-03-1867 - 29-04-1868	1Y 1M 1D	John Hay
Stanley	Sunderland	384		A.B.	30-05-1868 - 20-06-1869	1Y 0M 21D	Wilson Bros.
Amsterdam	Sunderland	731		A.B.	07-08-1869 - 18-11-1869	3M 11D	R.M.Hudson
Cornhill	Sunderland	339		A.B.	01-02-1870 - 12-09-1870	7M 11D	Wilson Bros.
Satanella	Dartmouth	198	Brigantine	Mate	21-10-1870 - 03-06-1871	7M 13D	T Clench Gallop
Mary	Sunderland			Mate	07-07-1871 - 24-01-1872	6M 18D	
Agincourt	London	443		Mate	14-02-1872 - 08-09-1874	2Y 5M 15D	Townsend Cator
Stirlingshire	Glasgow	549		Mate	12-01-1875 - 09-12-1875	10M 28D	Kerr Newton Co.
Corea	London	605	S.S	Mate	02-06-1876 - 20-11-1876	5M 20D	Parbury Watt
Evening Star	London	371		Mate	01-01-1877 - 28-02-1878	1Y 1M 28D	F Spring
Sophia- R- Luhrs	New York	661		Mate			J Zittlosen
George Shotton	Liverpool	556		Mate	11-12-1883 - 20-04-1884	5M 9D	Stewart & Co
River Garry	Glasgow	860	S.S.				Hargrove Hellon
Concordia	Glasgow	1,617	S.S.	Master			Donaldson Bros.
James Watt	Greenock	1,597	S.S.	Mate	17-10-1884 - 10-05-1885	6M 23D	Leich & Muir
Aboukir Bay	Glasgow	1,168	Barque 3 mast	Mate	10-07-1885 - 21-01-1889	2Y 5M 11D	Hatfield Cameron
Earl Of Dunmore	Glasgow	2,287	Barque 4 mast	Master	23-06-1891 - 09-03-1903	11Y 9M 4D	J D Thompson
Falls Of Garry	Sydney	2,087	Barque 4mast	Master	14-12-1903 - 18-04-1904	5M 4D	Wm. Kopsey
Criffel	Liverpool	1,250	Barque 3 mast	Master	03-08-1906 - 06-08-1907	1Y 0M 4D	McDiarmod & Co.

(No. 6980.)

"BUNINYONG" (S.S.)

AND

"CRIFFEL."

The Court of Marine Inquiry at Sydney.

In the matter of a formal inquiry held at Sydney before His Honour Judge Backhouse, assisted by John Mackenzie and Robert Laurie Boldchild, Assessors, into the circumstances attending the collision between the British ships "Buninyong" and "Criffel" in tow of the "Advance."

The Court, having carefully inquired into the circumstances attending the above-mentioned shipping casualty, comes to the decision following :—

1. The British ships "Buninyong" (Official No. 79538), and Criffel" (Official No. 97838), in tow of the "Advance" (Official No. 88922), were in collision near Robertson's Point, at the entrance to Mosman's Bay, an arm of Port Jackson, in the State of New South Wales, on the evening of the fourth day of May, 1906, when the "Buninyong" was inward bound from Melbourne, and the "Criffel" in tow of the "Advance," which had another vessel, the "Maroro," lashed alongside, was outward bound for Newcastle.

2. By such collision the British ships "Buninyong" and "Criffel" suffered serious damage.

3. The night was clear and moonlight, and the wind was from the north east.

4. As the "Criffel" was being towed out from Neutral Bay she was partly obscured to those on board the incoming "Buninyong" by the ship "Dione," which was anchored to the north of the fairway. The master of the "Buninyong" wrongly assumed that there was only one tow, and this mistake was partly the cause of the collision. It is also clear that the master of the "Advance" contributed to it, as the evidence shows that the length of line between the "Criffel" and his vessel was longer than was consistent with careful navigation, considering that tug and tows had to cross the fairway to get to their proper side. For this mistake the master of the "Advance" is principally to blame, but the pilot, and the master of the "Criffel," must share the responsibility with him.

120 Wt 35 9/1906 D & S 1 25875

5. While the Court is of opinion that both the master of the "Buninyong" and "Advance" are in fault, and also the master of the "Criffel," and the pilot, it does not call upon either of those chiefly to blame to show cause why his certificate of competency should not be suspended or cancelled for the following reasons:—The mistake of the master of the "Buninyong" was not an unnatural one as the regulation with regard to lights on tugs contemplates the tows being astern of the tug, and not one alongside and another astern; and the error of the master of the "Advance" is impliedly sanctioned by the Harbour Trust Regulation, which limits the length of line to be used between tug and tow in that part of the harbour to the westward of Fort Denison.

6. The Court has not been able to decide the actual distance between the stern of the "Advance" and the stern of the "Criffel," but, as stated above, it was clearly more than it should have been under the circumstances.

7. The Court is of opinion that the master of the "Buninyong" committed an error of judgment in going full speed ahead, instead of reversing, when he first saw the "Criffel." In all probability the additional strain on the tow rope by the impact of the bow of the "Buninyong" increased the violence of the blow with which the "Criffel" struck her.

8. The Court expresses the opinion that the regulation should limit the length of tow line anywhere inside the Heads.

9. The Court makes no order as to costs.

Dated this twenty-fourth day of July, 1906.

Alf. P. Backhouse,
Judge.

I, John Macvicar Anderson Bonthorne, registrar of the Court of Marine Inquiry at Sydney, hereby certify the foregoing to be a true copy of the decision of the Court in the matter of the inquiry into the circumstances attending the collision between the British ships "Buninyong" and "Criffel" in tow of the "Advance."

Dated at Sydney this twenty-sixth day of July, 1906.

J. M. A. Bonthorne,
Registrar of the Court.

(Issued in London by the Board of Trade on the 18th day of September, 1906.)

Documents supplied by Captain Joseph Kay

Captain Kay of the *Earl of Dunmore,* **is pictured in the centre of his afterguard.**
Photos supplied by Captain Joseph Kay

Left - Whilst under the command of Captain Kay, the *Earl of Dunmore* is seen here on fire in Sydney Harbour. The blaze which appears to be coming from the galley was extinguished.

Lowden, Edgar & Co

Candida

On Captain William Lowden's retirement from the sea, he struck up a business partnership with his Scottish counterpart John Edgar. The Liverpool based company was established in 1872 with Captain Lowden being the senior shareholder. In 1874 two ships *Greta,* and *Angerona* were built for the company, and these were followed by the Candida.
The partnership lasted until 1890, when Captain Lowden dissolved the firm and went on his own.

Angerona

Glenogil

The Port Glasgow ship building firm of Russells launched 34 vessels in the year 1891. Of these ships 6 were steamers whilst the other 28 were sail. One of these sailing vessels was the ***Glenogil***, a four masted barque built for John Edgar & Co of Liverpool.
After taking five months to build, the vessel was launched on 17 December 1891; the 2,286 gross ton ship's other dimensions were 279.6 x 42 x 24.3. Other measurements included the foc'sle of 28 feet and the poop deck 36 feet. She was not built with a Liverpool house; the sailors lived under the foc'sle head, whilst the officers, steward and any passengers lived aft.
The mast heights measured in feet from deck to truck, and from fore to jigger, were 150, 156, 154, and 122. The yards were interchangeable with the lower yards being 84 and the royals 48 feet.
After her launching in 1891, the ***Glenogil*** like so many other ships of sail was rigged and fitted out in a short space of time. Her first master was DR Stevenson, and he took the ship out to Sydney then across to San Francisco to load grain for Le Havre.
Her second voyage was from Cardiff to San Francisco, then back to Bristol from where she sailed for New York to load a cargo of case oil for Yokahama. Captain DR Stevenson died at sea in 1895. He was succeeded by Mr Davies the first mate; however, when the ship returned to the UK a year later, Captain D Jones took command. Later on a second Captain Stevenson became the ship's master, he stayed in the ship for seventeen years until January 1914.
When the second Captain Stevenson had joined the ***Glenogil*** in 1897, the vessel was loaded at Liverpool. The deadweight of 3,464 tons consisted of 2,564 tons of railway lines and 900 tons of general cargo. This comprised of 100 tons of ale and spirits, 36 mowing machines and a large number of mangles for Melbourne. Also on the manifest was a passenger named E Wynn-Morris, a youth who was making the voyage to improve his health. During the passage he took and developed a large number of photographs. (all of which were lost) and also kept a diary printed in 'The Nautical Magazine' Brown Son & Ferguson which described the daily events between Liverpool and Melbourne between 12 May and 2 Aug 1897.
Shortly after having left the Mersey when the sailors were stowing the deck gear away, a young stowaway named Pickering was discovered hiding beneath some old sails; the boy

was aged about fifteen. It was Captain Stevenson's intention to put him on any fishing boat that came close enough, but none did, and the young scouser made the passage. In all there were thirty three souls on board. The captain and his wife, three mates, six apprentices, a sail maker, carpenter, steward and cook made up the petty officers, whilst there were sixteen sailors and of course ... a stowaway! Pickering gave a good account of himself on the outward passage, and at a later date was reported to have joined a passenger ship in Melbourne as a cabin boy.

In the early part of 1914 and shortly before the start of WW1, the vessel was sold to the German firm of Krabbenhoft & Bock with a name change to ***Ernst.*** After loading a general cargo at Hamburg, the ship sailed for Australia under Captain Rienhold, but on arrival at Sydney, it was discovered with alarm by ***Ernst's*** captain, that Germany was at war with Britain and its Allies. The vessel was seized as a prize of war, and after discharging the cargo, her name was changed to ***Canowie,*** port of registry London, the ship's letters then became JLCQ.

Returning to the UK with a grain cargo, ***Canowie*** then loaded coal at Port Talbot. Sailing from the South Wales port in the summer of 1916 she was bound for Mejillones, but she was wrecked on Punta Pirulil Island de Chiloe on 9 October 1916.

The list below that came from the *Glenogil,* shows the weekly amount of victuals allowed to each crew member according to the Board of Trade scale of rationing. But it was only if and when such items could be obtained, as well as being at reasonable cost. On long voyages, flour based food quickly developed weevils in the tropical heat, and on long passages, fruit and vegetables were non-existent. There were no refrigerators on ships and only a few had ice rooms, therefore, fresh meat and vegetables only lasted a few days at best.

Bread - 7 pounds	Sugar - 14 ounces
Beef - 2 and one half pounds	Butter - 3 ounces
Pork - 2 pounds	Dried fruit - 4 ounces
Pressed Meat - 2 and one quarter pounds	Marmalade or Jam - One and one half pounds
Potatoes - 6 pounds	Molasses - Half of one pint
Vegetables - half of one pound	Water - 7 gallons
Flour - 2 pounds	
Peas - Two thirds of one pound	
Rice - Half of one pound	
Oatmeal - Half of one pound	
Tea - 1.75 ounces	
Coffee - 3.5 ounces	(per week)

The photograph of *Glenogil* shows her on 14 January 1892. Under the tow of two unidentified paddle wheeled tugs from Liverpool, the port to where she was bound to load her first cargo. The red ensign of all three vessels are flying at half mast to mark the death of the Duke of Clarence.

Photo by Captain Joseph Kay

Name	Position	Origin
A Stevenson	Master	Glasgow
Mrs Stevenson	Supernumerary	Glasgow
Brown	First Mate	Fife
McAlpine	Second Mate	Belfast
Young	Third Mate	Nottingham
E Wynne - Morris	Passenger	Llangollen
Dunlop	Apprentice	Fife
Lockley	Apprentice	Aldershot
Robinson	Apprentice	Nassau
Gahey	Apprentice	Fife
Brown	Apprentice	Blackpool
Hodges	Apprentice	India
?	Sailmaker	Germany
?	Carpenter	Russia
Owen	Cook	Liverpool
?	Steward	West Indies

Port Watch

Morley	Sailor	Auckland NZ
Henley	,,,,,,,,,	Queenstown Eire
Martin	,,,,,,,,,	Birkenhead
Kelly	,,,,,,,,,	Liverpool
Lindquist	,,,,,,,,,	Russia
Torfisson	,,,,,,,,,	Iceland
Johnsen	,,,,,,,,,	Russia
Christianson	,,,,,,,,,	Noorway

Starboard Watch

Whitfield	Sailor	Cumberland
Hayward	,,,,,,,,,	Warrington
Owen	,,,,,,,,,	Caernarfon
Johnsen	,,,,,,,,,	Stockholm
Haglan	,,,,,,,,,	Stockholm
Holmes	,,,,,,,,,	Russia
Galvinstrom	,,,,,,,,,	Russia
Alexander	,,,,,,,,,	New Orleans USA
Pickering	Stowaway	Liverpool

Birkdale

Captain Peter Iredale was a Cumberland seaman who began ship owning in 1864. His first of many fine vessels was the 496 ton iron barque ***Calabar.*** All his ships were registered in Liverpool, except the 800 ton ***Martha Fisher*** whose port of registry was Carlisle. Like so many other ship owners and retired sea captains, Captain Iredale lived in the Wirral on Merseyside. When John Porter of Londonderry married his daughter, a partnership was formed to become the Dale Line of Liverpool. To this extent, John Porter had business connections in Londonderry, and from then on, it was where many of the firm's ships were built. The *Birkdale* was one of those ships.

The three masted barque ***Birkdale*** was built at Londonderry in Biggers yard, then launched in 1892 for the Dale Line of Liverpool. Built of steel she was 248 feet in length and registered 1,483 gross tons. A smart little ship with a deadweight of 2,500 tons she was noted for some of her fine passages. In 1897 she was sold to Chadwick & Wainwright of Liverpool to be commanded by Captain JWS Davies. He stayed in the ship for 13 years until Captain RB Watts relieved him, then after a short while Captain Walmsley took command.

After hitting bad weather in 1912, the ***Birkdale*** was found in a helpless condition after having been adrift for 52 days. It was the French steamer ***Felix Touache*** which rescued and fed the starving crew, before aiding the battered ***Birkdale*** into refuge. Another point of interest occurred in 1922, when the ***Garthneil*** left Newcastle NSW with coal, arriving at her Callao destination 45 days later. On arrival at the Peruvian port, the town's dignitaries as well as the local band came to welcome the ship into port. In this most unusual set of circumstances, the townsfolk then heralded the crew as heroes. It later transpired that the community who'd been without flour for many months, had been told the ***Garthneil*** was the delivery ship. When the truth was later discovered that the ***Garthneil's*** cargo was in fact coal, the locals dropped their show of friendliness. However, a few days later when the delivery ship ***Birkdale*** did arrive with the wheat, it was their crew who were given the big welcome.

The ***Birkdale*** traded mostly in the Pacific, but after a long lay up the vessel was sold to a Callao firm in 1924. However, the new Peruvian owner kept the ship under the red ensign without a name change. In August 1924 when loaded with guano for Hull, and sailing from Callao on August 31, the little barque took quite a battering in the Pacific and put into Valparaiso for repairs. Leaving port she had an unpleasant passage via Cape Horn to Hull, and took a further 134 days to complete the passage. Although under foreign ownership, the ***Birkdale*** which flew the red ensign then became the topic of great concern in the House of Parliament; both with the length of her passage and the crew's nationalities.

In his book 'Last of the Windjammers' (Brown Son & Ferguson) Basil Lubbock states that her crew consisted of a Peruvian captain and second mate, an American mate, seven Germans, two Finns, one Briton, one Italian, one Swiss, one Peruvian, one Argentinian, one Norwegian and one Swede.

After discharging at Hull it was found there were no cargoes available, this resulted in the ship having another lengthy lay up. However, after gaining a charter and loading a cargo of coal from the Tyne, she sailed from the UK bound for Callao on 27 February 1927. Almost at the end of her passage fire broke out and the *Bikdale* finished up wrecked off Lobos Island. The Captain and 13 men were rescued in one boat by a Chilean warship. However the remaining six crew members in the other boat were never seen again.

Wanderer

Adapted from the poet John Masefield's 'The Wanderer of Liverpool' and supplied by Captain AW Kinghorn

The Liverpool shipbuilding firm of WH Potter was established in 1860, and they employed about 450 men in their Queen's Dock Island yard. It was a site where the Queen's Graving Dock was later built. In the years that followed the founding of his company, WH Potter became one of Liverpool's foremost ship builders with ships of sail being his speciality. When times were slack and like so many other yards of the day, Mr Potter often built a ship on speculation, then more often than not, sold his creation whilst it was still on the stocks. This method of working during slack times kept his men employed, whilst keeping his financial turnover on the move.

At times however, and due to lack of any realistic offers, those speculative Potter ships were not always sold on completion. Two of those vessels were the ***Wayfarer*** of 1886 and the ***Seafarer*** of 1888; therefore, Mr Potter operated those two ships himself. Those fine unsold vessels were followed by the ***Wanderer,*** a four mast steel barque that was laid down in August 1890, then launched twelve months later on 20 August 1891. The new ship was named by Mrs Potter the builder's wife. The ***Wanderer*** was a big ship with a gross tonnage of 2,903, her other dimensions were 308 x 46 x 25.8 feet. The ship had a central structure that many sailors called a Liverpool House, but because she was without a poop deck, her sailors referred to this midship structure or Liverpool House as the poop deck.

The original livery of the ***Wanderer*** was black topsides with a broad white band on which there were seventeen black painted gun ports. Beneath this she was French grey with a salmon boot topping; her masts and yards were buff as was her spike bowsprit. The figurehead was made by Liverpool's J&J Hammond, and this represented a woman gazing forward under an uplifted right hand shading her brow.

In keeping with the very latest practice for sailing vessels, the ***Wanderer*** was steered from amidships with chain and rod gear. These heavy but well greased chains ran along and beneath the main deck to the rudder. Like all similarly steered ships she was said to be heavy on the wheel, and when in bad weather she needed at least three men at the helm. At the after end in another wheel house, there was an emergency wheel beneath a whaleback stern. However, during the ship's lifetime this wheel was only connected on rare occasions. The four steel masts were of differing heights. The fore, main and mizzen were built in three sections with their t'gallant and royal masts being Oregon Pine. The mainmast truck with its skysail towered 174 feet above the deck. The 128 foot steel jigger was in one piece, and because she had no poop deck, the spanker had an extra large depth. After having been fitted out in the Queen's Dock, the ship was given a few hundred tons of coal for stiffening before towing over to Birkenhead for her first cargo. But that coal stiffening was loaded in the rain ... it was wet! and wet coal was well known for causing internal combustion and fire! ***Wanderer's*** first captain was fifty-two year old George Currie who hailed from Nova Scotia. His last ship the ***Wayfarer*** was one he'd commanded for five years. His new ship ***Wanderer*** then loaded coal at Birkenhead's West Float for San Francisco, the city where Captain Currie actually lived. The total complement for ***Wanderer's*** maiden voyage consisted of thirty seven. A generous number indeed! Of her twenty able seamen, the three Welshmen were the only Britons, whilst the other seventeen were all Scandinavian.

With loading complete and the ship ready to sail on 15 October 1891, a bout of bad weather hit the north west coast. Therefore, after being moved to the Alfred Basin, sailing

After losing her tug in heavy weather, *Wanderer* was towed into Kingstown by *SS Merannio.*

Author's Collection

was temporarily delayed. Then on Saturday the 17th, Mr Potter was on board to see his new ship begin her maiden voyage; but with one eye on the barometer, he suggested to his captain that sailing should be delayed until Monday the 19th. Most unfortunately for himself, the master mariner ignored his employer's advice.

Against a westerly wind the ***Wanderer*** began her maiden voyage by being towed into the river by the ***Wrestler,*** then out into the Liverpool Bay where the weather continued to worsen. Later on with Anglesey in sight amidst a howling westerly gale, the tug's captain suggested taking shelter in the lee of Holyhead, but Captain Currie declined the offer. Some time later whilst still under bare poles in St Georges Channel, the steel towing hawser carried away in the increasingly heavy weather. The ***Wrestler*** disappeared from view in the spume and spray, and all hands were ordered out to set the three lower topsails. However, most of those men were still suffering from the effects of their last drinking session. In the darkness, screaming winds and huge seas, those inebriated sailors tried to get the sails set. In one of his many poems, John Masefield described the situation on deck as chaotic. Loose sails with their chain sheets flying uncontrollably skywards, sparks from those same sheets showering the night sky, whilst the men staggered in deluges of water that came over the foc'sle head and bulwarks.

Mr and Mrs WH Potter
Photo Capt AW Kinghorn

Captain John Brander
Photo Capt AW Kinghorn

The lower topsails were eventually set, but with the coast too close for comfort, Captain Currie gave the order to wear ship.
With the helm hard up in huge seas and howling winds, the ship staggered in coming around, but as she did so, her three recently set heavy weather sails were ripped to shreds. The hurricane worsened! An attempt was then made to hoist red distress lights to the peak of the jigger gaff, but so bad had the weather become, that those not under command lights, as well as the spanker gaff to which they were attached, went clean over the side. Then blue lights and rockets were used! So loud was the scream of the of wind and the roar of the sea, that Captain Currie probably never heard the main skysail yard as it came crashing down upon him. At that particular time the captain was directing the midship wheel, but he was knocked unconscious by the falling skysail yard. Furthermore, half a dozen or so of his injured seamen were added to the list of casualties. Being not under command, getting thrown wildly about and rolling heavily in the pitch dark, the ***Wanderer*** was by that time in mortal danger! The after steering position was connected, for indeed the men who'd been on the midship wheel were terrified of the seas coming over the bridge deck. During the middle watch Captain Currie died of his injuries, but not before his calls for assistance were answered. Help came in the form of the ***SS Merannio,*** a steam coaster that stood by until daybreak until a chance to get a line across finally came. Time after time a tow was set up only for it to part. Most fortunately, the inclement weather abated and the sun came out. The tow to Kingstown in Ireland was finally made, then at a later date Captain Currie was buried in Dublin's Mount Jerome Cemetery. That storm in the Irish Sea was said to be the worst since 1863. After the tug ***Wrestler*** had lost her charge off South Arklow, and with herself being in some difficulty, she managed to bring the ***D Rice*** into Holyhead, where 200 craft of all types were taking refuge.
At Kingstown the damage to the ***Wanderer*** was assessed, and although there was no damage to her hull, she was a wreck aloft. The three wooden t'gallant masts had all gone, as had nine chain plates from the main rigging on the starboard side. The jigger head was bent, her spanker gaff, various spars and some of her sails were missing too.
Four days later, the ***Wrestler*** arrived at Kingstown to tow the battered ***Wanderer*** back to her builders in Liverpool. On arrival the ship was surveyed, repaired, and once again made ready for her maiden voyage ... with wet coal still in her hold! Captain John Brander then assumed command to recommence the passage to San Francisco.
After leaving Liverpool then rounding the Horn, and when about 1,000 miles short of her destination, the crew were under the impression the cargo was on fire, for indeed, the hull was unusually hot. Their suspicions were well founded, because after arriving at 'Frisco in March 1892, the sail maker saw smoke coming up from the 'tween decks. This was six months after that wet stiffening coal had been loaded in the Queen's Dock! After battling

to remove as much of the burning coal as possible, the ship was eventually set on a sandbank and flooded. Cargo was eventually discharged, then an enormous bill for repairs was presented to Captain Brander, before a cargo of grain was loaded. The ***Wanderer's*** destination was Queenstown for orders, a passage that took 110 days.

On arrival at Queenstown, and after laying at anchor for some weeks awaiting orders, the ***Wanderer*** was eventually towed to Liverpool. After having discharged her cargo she was once again surveyed in the Queen's Dock. The next voyage took the ***Wanderer*** from Liverpool to Philadelphia in ballast. On discharging her rubble, she was taken in tow by the tugs ***Samuel McCauley*** and ***Eva McCauley.*** However, more mishap occurred when the tow line parted; this resulted in the big four master being driven into a pier and wrecking it. From Philadelphia she took a cargo of case oil to Calcutta, then finished the voyage with a respectable 117 day run to Dundee with 22,870 bales of jute.

During a return visit to Philadelphia on 22 September 1896, her fourth voyage, Captain Brander left the ship to be replaced by Captain TS Tupman; he stayed in her until April 1901. To begin her sixth voyage starting at Bristol, the ***Wanderer*** saw the appointment of Captain Bailey. On passage to New York however, the weather was extremely heavy; the new captain took ill and had to leave the ship on arrival at the American port on 15 June

Shorn of her t'gallants in the Irish Sea, the battered *Wanderer* lays at Kingstown.

Author's Collection

1901. He was replaced by Captain Thomas Dunning at New York. The ship then went to Shanghai and Port Townsend before arriving at Tacoma. Whilst at this latter port, where eight sailors and the second mate fell victim to the wiles of the crimps, Captain Dunning had to pay $55 a head for replacements. Those newcomers to the foc'sle were a bad buy, and indeed, the new so-called second mate couldn't even navigate.

After having left that notorious crimping port for the UK, the ***Wanderer's*** first mate Mr Christian developed a severe problem from a former injury. His condition worsened to such an extent that he was in dire need of a doctor. In order for his chief officer to receive the required medical attention, Captain Dunning put his ship into the equally notorious crimping port of San Francisco.

The ship anchored in the bay, and it wasn't long before the crimp's runners made their presence felt. Before he departed ashore with the ailing Mr Christian however, the captain had armed his two senior apprentices with revolvers, with the express orders, that they were to shoot any crimps or their runners who attempted to come aboard.

Those two boys carried out their orders to the letter, until it went dark that is! In the meantime, Captain Dunning who'd been delayed at the hospital didn't arrive back until long after he anticipated. Consequently, the nine men he'd shipped at Tacoma had all gone down the anchor cable and into the runner's boat. It's not known whether these deserting drop outs were replaced, but the passage back to the UK once again took an admirable 110 days. The next voyage saw the ***Wanderer*** sailing once again in ballast for Philadelphia. From there she took 120,000 cases of oil to Kobe before crossing the Pacific to Tacoma. She must have been a happy ship, because there was only one case of desertion. That man was tempted into the runner's boat, then at a later date sold back to the ship for $35. But there was to be yet another incident of wrong doing whilst the ship was at anchor in the bay. In conjunction with some of the sailors, a thief boarded the ship and stole a quantity of paint. However, the theft was immediately discovered, and those involved were apprehended and locked up ashore.

Whilst off Cape Horn on the homeward passage, the $35 seaman who'd previously deserted sent word to the captain, that he was unable to work due to sore feet. Captain Dunning then went into the sailor's foc'sle, and after finding nothing wrong with the complainant promptly ordered him to turn to. The rebellious sailor then attacked his master, but Captain Dunning was more than able to take care of his assailant. Later on the mutinous bosun fought with the second mate and an able seaman, before eventually refusing to work at all.

That unpleasant voyage ended at Cardiff where the ***Wanderer*** took charge of her tug whilst shifting ship. She then collided with the ***SS Strathmore.*** The steamer's fore topmast was bent, whilst the ***Wanderer*** suffered damage to some of her head gear.

The ship's eighth voyage was from Cardiff with a cargo of coke, this was topped up in the 'tweens with general at Antwerp. Destination San Francisco! Due to bad weather, the ship was first held up for a few days in St Helen's Bay, Isle of Wight. Then after sailing down channel was again forced to take refuge, this time in the Carrick Roads of Falmouth where she stayed for a week. Captain Dunning then took his ship around The Cape of Good Hope, in a passage that took 155 days.

On board for the voyage was the usual poultry and pigs. Those hens were excellent layers,

Wanderer *Author's Collection*

for indeed, on every one of the 155 day run they produced eggs. The ***Wanderer*** must have been a good feeder too, because with all the left over food from the galley, her two pigs weighed in at 180 and 120 pounds.

Early in the passage the Irish sail maker had a set to with the Negro cook. The Irishman then ordered his adversary from the petty officer's round house, and for the rest of the trip, the evicted man lived in the galley or slept out on deck. There is no record as to what the nature of the cook's offence had been. On arrival at San Francisco whilst laying close in, the ship's bowsprit was pointing over the wharf; on the following morning, it was discovered that a six foot string of bones were hanging from the ***Wanderer's*** bowsprit. It

appears that this was a derogatory reminder from the sailors of a nearby American ship, that British ships were ill found and hungry. However, there were no reported incidents of desertion during that voyage under Captain Dunning.
After discharging the general cargo from her 'tweens, the ship was towed up the Sacramento River to discharge her Welsh coke. Then after a few week's lay up, ports were cut into her bows and she sailed in ballast for Port Blakely. Huge baulks of timber were then hauled through the ports with wire ropes, and later on a deck cargo of timber was secured. On conversing with the sawmill hands, the ***Wanderer's*** sailors learned that most of them were former seamen. Men who'd deserted their ships some years previous in the Californian gold rush. Their pay and conditions in the lumber camp were excellent, and the temptation to join them by deserting was a strong one indeed. On passage back to the Mersey, the deck capstans had been covered up by the deck cargo. The sailors then had to use 'Norwegian Steam' for indeed, to swing those lower yards around without the capstans proved a most difficult and back breaking job.
On arrival at Liverpool, the cargo was said to be the finest consignment of timber ever to have been brought into the port. To complete her discharge, the ***Wanderer*** was then towed around to Cardiff where she was by that time becoming a regular visitor. The ship was dry-docked before towing to Antwerp for a general cargo. On learning that his discharging port was once again San Francisco, Captain Dunning who'd remained in command, decided once again to run east. After leaving the Belgian port the ***Wanderer*** arrived at 'Frisco on 22 April 1906. Some days before arriving at San Francisco the crew mutinied. The carpenter, sail maker, starboard bosun, twenty able seamen and two ordinary seamen all refused to work. As a consequence, it took the master, two mates, four apprentices, port bosun and the steward to shorten sail and bring her in. On passing the Golden Gate, it transpired that two days previous to their arrival, the great earthquake of 1906 had struck the city.
No tugs were available due to their giving assistance in fighting the fires, and on the following day, those who'd mutinied deserted ship. The ship then received a nice cargo of honey, tinned fruits, and orders for Queenstown. On the passage home to the UK, the ***Wanderer*** raced with four other ships, the ***Ellisland, Latimer, Gael***, and the Norwegian ***Prince Robert***. The eventual winner was the ***Wanderer,*** despite becoming partly dismasted during the passage!

Regarding that mishap, one of the Wanderer's sailor's gave the following account.

'Coming home from 'Frisco we had light winds until 5 degrees north of the line, and that's where we lost our fore t'gallant mast. There was a huge swell running and we were

heading right into it. Braced sharp up on a starboard tack in light winds, the ship pitched heavily and took deluges of water over the foc'sle head. This resulted in the strain on the masts and braces being quite heavy.
At about 8.30 am a white squall suddenly descended upon us. Most fortunately, Captain Dunning who was on deck sang out,
"Lower away the skysail and royal halyards."
At that very moment she took a huge sea over the foc'sle head. The mass of water roared down the deck, and the man at the fore royal halyard unsurprisingly ran away. The ship heeled over in the squall, took another plunge, and the fore t'gallant mast snapped like a carrot at the cap. The mainmast itself was situated in line with the forepart of the bridge deck, or Liverpool house, therefore, all its shrouds, backstays and running gear were on the bridge deck. I was watch below at the time, but in the commotion ran up on deck to hear the captain exclaim,
"Look, the main t'gallant's going too."
I jumped to the skysail halyard, whilst Captain Dunning himself lowered the royal yard half down. Although the main t'gallant mast was saved, it was so badly splintered at the heel it was of no further use. The chief officer then had to chase the sailors back to work as they'd all taken refuge in the terrifying situation.
A Sydney Larrikin shipped at 'Frisco was having a rough time of it, and all due to him being an incompetent slacker. Nevertheless, it was he who slid out on the lee topsail yardarm, went down the backstay, and then cut the crane line with his knife. We watched anxiously, expecting him to be hurled to the deck as the weight came off the backstays. Due to his efforts however, the whole tangled mess of wire, rope and sail then went into the sea, and indeed, the Sydney Larrikin emerged without a scratch. I remember the captain saying
"Well that blighter's a damn good man after all." After that heroic episode, the 'Sydney Larrikin' as he was called, had a much easier time of it.
At a later date when we were 26 north, the replacement fore t'gallant mast was again lost. However, although the ***Wanderer*** had to finish her passage under topsails and courses, she still beat her four competitors in the race. The ship eventually arrived to pick up a tug at Dungarvan after being 153 days out. On arrival at Liverpool for an overhaul, it was then discovered that an 86 foot replacement for her main t'gallant mast could not be obtained. There just wasn't a spar that long anywhere in the UK, and neither could one of even 76 feet be found. Therefore, the Wanderer was shorn of her pride … her glorious main skysail!
After discharge, the ship which by that time had been painted grey, was towed to the Altenbruch Roads by the ***Sarah Jolliffe.*** That tow to Hamburg was then completed by the

German tug ***Lome,*** Captain Dunning had his wife aboard for the passage, and the ***Wanderer*** anchored in the River Elbe at 4.30 pm on 13 April 1907. On the pilot's instructions, anchor lights were hoisted at 7.15 pm. The aftermost one at the peak of the gaff 20 feet up, whilst the forrard one was placed 35 feet up on the fourth swifter of the starboard foremast shrouds … and not on the forestay as was the norm! With the second mate and one seaman doing the anchor watch, the lights were checked at regular intervals with the usual report of "Lights are bright and all's well."

At 9 pm the Austral liner ***SS Hagen*** anchored close to the ***Wanderer*** and turned all her electric lights and deck clusters on. A pilot who was going down river a little later, testified at the enquiry that the lights from the ***SS Hagen*** were so bright, that he failed to notice those of the ***Wanderer***. Other pilots who also bore witness gave varying accounts of the luminosity of the sailing vessel's anchor lights.

However, the 6,331 ton ***SS Gertrud Woermann,*** which had recently disembarked over 600 troops at Cuxhaven, was then steaming at over 14 knots for her next port of call at Brunsbuttel. The time was 1.45 am on 14 April 1907. At that time, the twin screw steamer had two pilots, its captain and his second mate on the bridge. The seaman lookout who should have been up in the crows nest, was in fact working on the afterdeck tidying up. Indeed, it was the ***Gertrud Woermann's*** helmsman who first saw and reported the lights of the ***Wanderer*** right ahead. The pilots had been under the impression the lookout was in the crow's nest, and at the time they were studying some distant navigational beacon.

"Hard to port … full astern both engines."

Came the order from the pilot. But alas. Too late! The steamer struck the sailer on the port bow abaft of her collision bulkhead.

Captain Dunning in company with others then came running up to the bridge deck. The rush of water could be heard coming through the hold ventilators, and on realising his ship was doomed, the captain gave the dreaded order.

"Swing the boats out and abandon ship."

Thanks to the captain's cool handling of the affair, there was no panic. His wife was put aboard the passenger ship's tug that had been following astern, and after all the understandable commotion, the starboard boat was launched and all hands were saved. Drifting around in the dark for some time, the tug ***Fair Play V*** picked up the survivors and landed them all at Cuxhaven.

At daylight on the 14th, it was found that the wreck of the ***Wanderer*** was laying on her side in 24 feet of water … on a quicksand bottom! At first it was thought the ship could be saved, but by the 16th she'd settled so far in the quicksand there was no hope of salvage whatsoever.

At the court of enquiry held at Hamburg on 22 April 1907, it was deemed by Admiral von

Bodenhausen, that the fault of the collision lay entirely with the command of the ***Gertrud Woermann.*** That ship's defence was the anchor lights of the stricken vessel were inadequate, and couldn't be seen until the last minute. Then at the Court of the Landgericht on 3 December 1907, the owners of the ***Gertrud Woerman*** were ordered to pay £18,055 in damages, as well as £976 15s 0d for the crew's personal effects.

……………………..

Although the poet John Masefield did serve briefly at sea in sail … albeit for a short time, it is not known if he actually served on the *Wanderer*.

The Wanderer of Liverpool

Photo - Captain AW Kinghorn

Ships of sail moored in tiers at the Peruvian port of Iquiqui.
James Maguire

Seen here under the charge of a Cock Tug, the five masted Danish barque *Kobenhavn* tows down the River Mersey. Built by Ramage & Ferguson of Leith for the East Asiatic Co of Copenhagen, this 3,901 ton vessel was designed as a cargo carrying cadet ship. Originally launched in 1916, the British government commandeered her before completion, named her *Black Dragon,* then used her as an oil hulk at Gibralter. A second ship's hull was then built in 1921 resulting in the vessel shown above. However, after leaving Buenos Aires for Melbourne in ballast on 14 Dec 1928, *Kobenhavn* disappeared with a complement of sixty.

Anchored in the Mersey awaiting the tide, is the German barque *Priwall.* Completed in 1919 for the Flying P Line of Hamburg, she was first used in the WCSA nitrate trade, then converted to a cargo carrying cadet ship in 1926. During WW2 she was gifted to the Chilean government for fear of being sunk by the Allies and re-named *Lautaro.* When she left Iquique with nitrates for San Francisco in Feb 1945, her complement of 183 were mostly Chilean cadets. Fire broke out in the cargo and the 3,185 ton vessel became a total loss. Twenty of her crew were lost in the blaze.

Lwow

One of the many sailing vessels owned by T&J Brocklebank was the *Chinsura*. She was 1,266 tons, built of iron by RG Glover at Birkenhead, and launched in April 1865. Sold to R Hughes of Liverpool in 1883, she remained with them until 1893 when sold to the Italians and renamed *Lucco*. Dismasted five years later, the vessel was sold to Landberg & Zoon of Batavia. Cut down to a barque, her name then changed to *Nest*. After trading in the far east for many years, Van Meel of Rotterdam became her next owner in 1920. However, after only one year she once again changed hands and flags, this time to the Polish Government. Her name then became *Lwow,* with an engine installed she was used for sail training. In 1929 she was broken up to make way for the new sail training vessel *Dar Pomorza.*

Kruzenstern

The *Kruzenstern* pictured above, was named after the first Russian to circumnavigate the globe. The ship itself was originally the Padua of Hamburge and belonged to the famous Flying P Line *of* Ferdinand Laeiz. Built at Wesermunde and launched on 24 June 1926, the 3,064 ton barque came from the yard of JC Tecklenborg. Also used as a cargo carrying cadet ship, she traded mainly to Chile for nitrates and Australia for wheat. Laid up at Flensburg during WW2, the *Padua* was used as a Kreigsmarine accommodation ship. At the end of the war she was seized by the Russians for use as a sail training vessel and given the name of *Kruzenstern.* Still in use as a cadet ship she is a regular visitor to the Mersey during the 'Tall Ship' races.'

The Port of Liverpool Past and Present

In being little more than a fishing village, Liverpool was once regarded as rather unimportant. Indeed, so insignificant was its status, that it wasn't even included in the sixteenth century Ptolemy map of England. In those times the ancient city of Chester was the North West's major seaport, whilst the River Dee was the main waterway to the region.

Between the years 1207 to 1709, Lyverpoole, as it was then spelt, was controlled by a borough acting under a special act of parliament. However, from 1709 onwards that borough began losing its influence on the merchants, the port slowly expanded and eventually overtook Chester as the North West's main seaport. Then Bristol was overtaken to make the Merseyside port the principal shipping centre of the west coast. In its growing importance it also passed the ports of Spain and Portugal in the African and American trades, or to put it differently, the slave trade. The Goree that is opposite the Liver Buildings was the trading area for slaves and the remains of ringbolts on some of the buildings can still be seen.

Before the beginning of the nineteenth century, the people of Liverpool spoke with a Lancashire accent. But when in the first half of the century a multitude of Irish immigrants arrived in Liverpool to escape their crop failures, there were as many Irish as English in the port of Liverpool. Consequently, the languages were crossed resulting in a now unmistakable 'Scouse' accent.

By 1857 the borough had completely lost its authority in control of the port, the result being the formation of The Mersey Docks & Harbour Board. This was the organisation that assumed responsibility for the creation of Liverpool's docks. The MD&HB were also responsible for the building of numerous warehouses and bridges as well as the dredging of the river. After the middle of the nineteenth century Liverpool had grown dramatically in its progression, and indeed, it was Jesse Hartley who played a major part in the design and structure of the docklands. During the 19th century especially, Liverpool was the main port used in the migration of Europeans to the Americas. Indeed, there are many Americans of today, whose ancestors travelled from Liverpool to New York on ships of both steam and sail. That migratory practice continued more than half way into the twentieth century, when the passenger liners of the Cunard White Star and Canadian

Pacific were instrumental in ferrying hundreds of thousands of the migrants from Liverpool to America and Canada.

Liverpool played an enormous part in both World Wars and especially WW2, the port was then the home base of the Western Approaches. Of the many anti-submarine warships that frequented the Mersey, the famous sloop HMS ***Starling*** was adopted by the Borough of Bootle.

Towards the end of the 20th century, and after having been one of the worlds busiest seaports, the Liverpool docks has since adopted an appearance of emptiness and desolation. Long gone are the days of the early 19th century, when a sailing ship filled every quay side berth, their elegant jib-booms run in, and their towering masts silhouetted against the sky. Those were the days when just about every shipboard task was performed with aid of a sea shanty. With the disappearance of the sailing ships and the beginning of the 20th century, both the sea shanties and the men of sail also faded into oblivion.

Then came the dominance of the steamships, when palls of smoke from the coal burning ships filled the city's atmosphere. There was also the accompanying smoke from factory chimneys and houses, and this blackened the buildings for miles around.

Cargo handling on ships had been much improved, and the scene at every dock was one of great activity. Indeed, with cranes and derricks handling cargoes amidst the clattering hiss of the steam winches, work went on by day and night. Those were the days when thousands of dockers were employed to handle the cargoes of the port, and also the large numbers of seamen who were engaged to carry those same cargoes to and from every corner of the globe. As well as the dock workers and seamen, there are also many other Merseysiders who owe their livelihood to the existence of the shipping industry.

In modern times however, and although most of the quay sides are devoid of ships, the Port of Liverpool is handling more goods than ever before. It is now the container ships and VLCCs (Very large crude carriers) that have since taken over. They fill the Seaforth Container Terminal at the north docks, and it is these huge 50,000 ton ships which now bring the cargoes to and from the port. The other berths which are further south now have their sheds falling into disrepair, and the quay-sides are in part overgrown with grass and weeds. The great passenger liners have all gone, as have the cargo liners and the tramp steamers.

Many people in Liverpool still talk about the great Merchant Navy we once had, of the thousands of merchant seamen who came from the port, then wonder how the service was allowed to fade away into the history books. At one time there was hardly a house in the city, that didn't have a seaman, a dock worker or someone else living within its walls who earned their living from ships. The explanation of the now vanished profession of the seaman and their ships is quite simple to explain, and in reality can be explained in just

Looking south down Liverpool's South Castle Street in 1907, with the domed Custom House of Canning Place in the background. Out of sight and to the left of the Custom's House is the Sailor's Home, whilst to its right are the Salthouse and Canning Docks.

By the year 1907 the transformation of sail to steam was almost complete. Ships of sail were becoming an increasing rarity, and crews for such were hard to find. Seamen of the day opted for the steamships, which by that time were more reliable and comfortable.

one word. 'Modernization.'
At the turn of the 20th century, the berths at the Liverpool docks were usually full with ships of both sail and steam. But so slow was a ship's turn around time in those days, in comparison with today, that many vessels arriving from abroad would have to anchor at the Mersey Bar and await a vacant berth. The merchant ships of the year 1900 registered much less in tonnage than those of later times, and taking for example a sailing ship like the ***California***, this vessel could carry a cargo of about 4,800 tons. At the same time, a large number of British foreign going steamships were about the same size. To discharge, then load a general cargo on one of these average sized ships would possibly take a month or even more.
On the other hand, with all the latest cargo handling techniques that is now in place, a ship of today would be able to discharge and load ten times as much in just a few days and that's to say nothing of the oil tankers. The result of years of progression and modernisation, is that a high speed container ship or bulk carrier of 50,000 tons, can now manage with a crew of just twenty men, whereas the aforesaid 3,000 ton ship ***California*** needed a crew of over thirty.
In recent years Liverpool has become a tourist attraction with regard to its great maritime past. This has been deliberated by one of the warehouses in the Albert Dock, and one that has been converted into a maritime museum. Visitors to this magnificent building are probably aware of its once being a warehouse built in the middle of the nineteenth century, and one that was used for storing the import and export cargoes for vessels of both steam and sail. This building like so many other dockside warehouses, was in fact due for demolition some years ago. It has been said however, that because it had been so massively and solidly constructed, the cost of razing it to the ground was estimated as more than the cost of refurbishing it. Therefore, this and many more of these old warehouses have survived to be transformed into offices, apartments, hotels, restaurants and of course a maritime museum. There appears to be no doubt at all, that if these warehouses are left alone, they'll still be standing for many centuries yet to come.
As the visitors to the Maritime Museum in the Albert Dock cast their eyes around, they'll be able to see many of the nautical landmarks that have survived the years. There are the half tide locks and its gates, as well as the pump-house which once provided the power to fill and empty those locks, there are the swing bridges which opened and closed at regular intervals to allow the passage of the sailing ships. There are also an abundance of bollards and ring-bolts on the quay-side to which the berthing ropes of those ships of sail were once secured.
When one looks along the dock road to the south, the business of the port's oldest ship chandler Joseph P Lamb can be seen. This company situated in Wapping, is just a short

walk along the dock road from the Albert Dock, and indeed, that firm was established long before the first steamships were ever built. JP Lamb specialised then, just as they do today, in ship chandlery and sail-making. This was the firm that supplied the great sailing ships of the past; items that included ropes, sails, paint, and victuals, in fact every single item imaginable that's required to keep a ship at sea. Some of these ships included the fabulous 'Liverpool Yankee Clippers' as well as the first steamships to ever use the port. In their office which is clearly advertised on their building walls, JP Lamb have their own maritime museum. However, many of the artifacts, relics, and account ledgers which had been with the company for over two hundred years, have since been donated to the Merseyside Maritime Museum.

Behind the establishment of Joseph P Lamb and clearly visible from the Albert Dock, lays another large warehouse with a nautical past; its owner's name and business painted upon its walls - Heaps Rice Mill. This company that were also ship-owners in the 19th century, were then known as the Heaps Thames & Mersey Line. Some of their vessels which were - all sailing ships - included the *Antiope, Marpesia, Theopane, Cassiope, Parthenope and Melanope.* In the transportation of rice to their Liverpool mills, they traded mainly to Burma and other far eastern ports. Although they still continued in rice milling today, Heaps sold their fleet off to the Liverpool firm of Gracie Beazley in 1882.

Adjacent to the Albert Dock is the Salthouse Dock, and right outside the entrance of this half tide dock lies the legendary 'Canning Place' and 'Paradise Street.' These thoroughfares have been the subject of many a sea shanty, where Maggie May and her like preyed and took advantage of many a sailor's hard earned money. In Canning Place the remains of the Sailors Home lies at its junction with Paradise Street. Looking north from the Albert Dock, one can see the elegant Port of Liverpool Buildings, the Cunard Buildings and the Liver Buildings; structures that were completed in the early part of the twentieth century. Then there is the India Buildings in Water Street, a structure built by George Holt, the father of Alfred Holt, founder of the Blue Funnel Line. Since it was completed in the mid 19th century, this building has been the head office for countless shipping companies large and small. Just a stone's throw from there is the Liver Buildings, whilst a few yards further to the south of these buildings, the house flag of T&J Harrison proudly flies in Covent Garden. Due to their funnel markings, this is the shipping company that acquired the famous pseudonym of 'two of fat and one of lean.' Nevertheless, and since its founding, that same company has itself been struck by its own pseudonym. Indeed, during both World Wars it had endured more lean years than fat ones. However, and at the time of writing they have survived, furthermore, and during the company's existence, they've provided employment for countless thousands of men both at home and abroad. They also have their company museum, and its keeper; Captain

Graeme Cubbin, has over the years acquired quite a collection of company relics, and there are plenty of them, for indeed, T&J Harrisons have been in existence for almost two centuries. (T&J Harrisons have since ceased to exist.)
Just a few yards through Covent Garden to the north stands the church of St. Nicholas - otherwise known as the sailor's church. On the Pier Head which is between the Liver Buildings and the landing stage are the monuments to the many thousands of seamen who lost their lives performing their duty in the Mercantile Marine and Merchant Navy.

The Sailor's Home in Liverpool

Liverpool County Museum

Built by Russell of Glasgow in 1896 for CA Walker, the 1,109 ton *Sound of Jura* is pictured under tow in the River Mersey. In 1916 she was fitted with an engine which enabled her to make three knots in a calm. Purchased by the Kerguelen Whaling and Sealing Company she ran from Cape Town supplying the whaling fleet with coal. She was broken up on the beach at Simonstown in 1927.

The Liver Buildings might be Liverpool's best known landmark today. But before the turn of the 20th century the Custom's House seen here laid claim to the honour. The Custom's House was bombed beyond repair during WW2.

Four mast ships were frequent visitors to the Mersey. The ship named Liverpool was a four master

Author's Collection

Whoever this Liverpool sailor was, he was number nineteen on the ship's articles.

Left - Bidston Hill Light House. The signal station that acted as a lookout to alert the Liverpool authorities of a ship's arrival.

The famous anti-submarine sloop HMS Starling was adopted by the Borough of Bootle. Her group once sank six submarines in one patrol. Despite strenuous efforts to save her for Bootle, she was scrapped after serving as a training ship in the 1950s

In this mid nineteenth century portrayal of the Liverpool landing stage, a paddle wheeled Mersey Ferry steams against the wind and downstream towards her Birkenhead destination. The Saint Nicholas Church otherwise known as The Sailor's Church is visible on the left, whilst to the right, the masts of numerous sailing vessels can be seen in the Canning and Salthouse Docks. ***Liverpool County Museums***

The White Star Line

The origins of this famous shipping company began in 1852, when John Pilkington and Henry Threlfall-Wilson formed the White Star Line of sailing packets. The two Lancashire men were already experienced in ship broking, and they could see that trade to the Antipodes had a great future.
Therefore, they purchased and sent their first ship ***Tantivy*** out to Australia. Business flourished and with good management and an equal share of good fortune, the company grew rapidly. So fast did it grow in fact, that within three years and in conjunction with the Black Ball Line of Liverpool, the White Star Line had secured part of the mail contract for the delivery of mails to Australia.
The contract, which had been negotiated by James Baines of the Black Ball Line, had stipulated that each mail ship must arrive at Melbourne from the UK within 65 days, and for every day over, a penalty of £100 would be incurred.
The White Star Line had some fast ships, and the ones selected to carry the mails were the ***Shalimar, Emma, Mermaid, Fitzjames*** and ***Ben Nevis,*** as well as their own two Liverpool Yankee Clippers ***White Star*** and ***Red Jacket.*** Things went well at the start, but unfortunately the mail contract proved to be too much with the £100 a day forfeits. Just like the Black Ball Line, the company only lasted as long the Australian gold rush was in progress, and when that was finished so were they. But most unfortunately the mail contract was still in force. White Star also suffered dreadful luck in the way some of their ships came to grief. Out of a total of 45 ships which the company owned, 23 were lost in various ways.
The company's interests were then sold to the Shaw Saville & Albion Co in 1867, whilst the famous house flag and the remaining ships went to Thomas Ismay of Liverpool. Ismay then became the owner of the White Star Line. In 1870 Ismay joined up with William Imrie, and in the same year the company ordered their first screw steamship. That vessel was the **SS *Oceanic*** of 3,808 tons built by Harland & Wolff of Belfast; its dimensions were, 420 x 40.9 x 23.4.
The ship was a modern wonder by incorporating all the latest unheard of luxuries for passengers. She was also fast, her length and breadth ratio of over ten to one gave her a speed of 14 knots. To compliment her double expansion steam engines, she was also sail assisted with the rig of a four mast barque. Although Ismay and Imrie owned sailing vessels, and for them to avoid paying extra taxes, the new steamer was known as

belonging to the Oceanic Steamship Company. On the ***Oceanic's*** maiden voyage which began on 2 March 1871, she was advertised in the Liverpool Daily Post. In that advert, the cost of a single saloon passage to New York was 18 guineas, and the round trip 27 guineas. In 1874 the liner returned from her transatlantic travels to her builders for alterations, the four masts were shortened and she had two additional boilers installed to her existing 12. On completion of her refit, the ***Oceanic*** went through the Suez Canal and out to the Far East. This was to inaugurate a service that ran between Hong Kong, Yokohama and San Francisco. During the following years, with the ***Oceanic*** out in the Far East, Ismay & Imrie's Oceanic Steamship Company also operated a high class passenger service to North America.

In 1879 the ***Oceanic*** was once more back in Belfast where she was given a refit lasting four months; the vessel then returned to San Francisco, where on arrival in June 1880, she continued with the passenger trade. By this time the ***Oceanic*** had built up a great reputation in the Pacific, and she remained on the service for a further 15 years.

White Star

From a painting by Terry Callan

In 1895 however, the ship which was now 24 years old was badly in need of another re-fit, she therefore returned to the builder's yard at Belfast. On arrival at Queens Island Yard, where new engines were to be installed, it was decided by the company that the refit wouldn't be feasible after all. This was mainly due to the age of the ship. They also decided against selling her to another company, simply because, after she'd built up such a huge reputation both at home and abroad, her transfer to another company may tarnish the company image. The real reason of course, was that if she eventually fell into the wrong hands she may be used as a tramp steamer. It was therefore decided that the ***Oceanic*** should be scrapped.

Just like the Cunard Line, the White Star Line continued to expand. However, the loss of their ship ***Titanic*** on 15 April 1912, was only one of the catastrophes that later beset the company, they also had their misfortunes in ship losses during World War One, as well as having to fight off fierce competition from all the leading European nations.

Oceanic

California

The model of the *California* that lay in the lounge of the Liverpool Sailor's Home. On the demolition of that building, it was presented to the Liverpool County Museum.

Liverpool County Museum

Author's Collection

California

The four mast barque *California* towing up the River Mersey to end her maiden voyage. To discharge her cargo of San Francisco grain, the pilot has decided to berth the ship starboard side to the quay; for this reason, the lower yards have been braced around to port. By bracing those lower yards around, it lessens the chance of any obstructions on the quayside, for if the yards were squared, they'd protrude over the ship's sides by about twenty six feet on each side. It also gives free passage for any waterborne craft with right of way to pass on her port side. The t'gallants and royal yards have not been braced around as they won't present any problem, for as well as being shorter, they'd be some 100 feet or more above the deck level and well clear of any workings. In some cases however, the main yard may be swung around the opposite way and over the quayside, for it was quite often the practice for those lower yards to be used as derricks for loading light stores and cargoes, and especially in some foreign ports where cargo handling techniques were primitive.

California

Like so many of the big companies that ran steamships, the Oceanic Steamship Company, otherwise known as The White Star Line, wanted their cadets to be sail trained, therefore, they had the ***California*** built. Coming from the same plans as the ***Sindia, Holkar,*** and ***Lord Templemore,*** the ***California*** was the largest sailing vessel ever owned by Ismay & Imrie. Their intention was to use her in their North West Shipping Company as a cargo carrying cadet ship.

By this method, the company cadets were able to receive the best of instruction and education, whilst the ship's earnings made a contribution towards its upkeep. The plan was for ***California*** to make one round the world voyage each year, taking as well as her normal crew, a large new class of cadets. Barque rigged, the four mast ***California*** with her double topsails, double t'gallants and royals had a length between perpendiculars of 329 feet, a beam 45 feet and a depth of nearly 27 feet. Another of her features was, that as she was a training vessel, reef points were added to her courses and upper topsails. Reef points were by that time a thing of the past on the last ships of sail. Their exclusion was because sailing ship crews were kept at a bare minimum, there just weren't enough sailors on ships to warrant their being. However, on a training ship things were different, there were plenty of hands, and the reefing of sails would enhance the seamanship education of the young officers to be.

The ***California*** never set any sailing records, and like her sister ships she was generally regarded as being a slow coach. On her maiden voyage from Liverpool to San Francisco however, she did make the passage in 130 days. This was regarded as most satisfactory for a maiden voyage, a time when all kinds of teething problems were liable to erupt. However, on the homeward run back to Liverpool with a full load of grain, she made an even better passage of 121 days.

As far as the training ship scheme went, the White Star Line's plans didn't seem to be working out at all, because in 1895 the ***California*** was sold to Ritson & Livesly another Liverpool firm. On purchasing this extremely well maintained vessel, the new owners removed all the extra cadet accommodation, then after just one voyage in 1897, they sold her at a handsome profit to the German firm of Slomans. She was renamed ***Alster*** and registered in Hamburg. In 1898 the vessel was sold on yet again, this time to Schramm another Hamburg Ship owner. Like so many other German ships, the ***Alster*** was given the traditional rig of double gaff sails on her jigger mast. She then began trading to the West

Coast of South America (WCSA) taking general cargoes out, and bringing nitrates back to Germany.

At some time during Schramm's ownership the ***Alster*** was fitted with the currently popular brace winches. In 1912 the ship was sold to Vinnens, another German firm who renamed her ***Christel Vinnen***, she then made a couple more trips to the WCSA. However, when the ship left Hamburg for Valparaiso in 1914, it was to be for the last time, for on her arrival at the Chilean port, it was discovered that the declaration of war between Britain and Germany had taken place.

The ***Christel Vinnen*** was therefore in enemy territory. She was seized by the authorities and her crew interned. Before the crew were removed from their ship however, they made great efforts to render the ship as un-seaworthy as possible. Indeed, they smashed everything they could on the decks and apparently made a good job of it, because for the rest of the war the vessel could only be used as a hulk.

Three years after the Great War had ended in 1922, the ship was given to Italy as a reparation of war. Although the hull was found to be in good condition, her deck gear which included the brace winches had been so badly damaged, that the ship was sold for what she was worth as scrap. In 1926 another owner emerged and had the barque repaired and put back into service; her new captain was Thomas Kirkwood.

After almost 5,000 tons of nitrates had been loaded into his ship, Captain Kirkwood sailed for Norfolk, Virginia. However, instead of going around Cape Horn, her new captain decided to take his ship through the Panama Canal, a route which would save both time and money. But it was a mistake, because on leaving port the ***Christel Vinnen*** was so long in the windless zones of the Pacific trying to reach the Panama Canal, that she was posted missing. When she did show up and took a tow through the Panama Canal, the fee was so high that the voyage wasn't going to show a profit.

However worse was to come - much worse! On passing through the Panama Canal she made her way north towards Norfolk, then as she was almost at her destination, and not so far away from the spot where her sister ship ***Sindia*** had come to grief, ***Christel Vinnen*** ran aground on Providence Isle on 15 April, 1927. Although the whole of her crew were rescued, the four mast barque became a total loss.

T&J Brocklebank

Daniel Brocklebank was the son of a clergyman born in 1741 at the little Cumberland village of Morland. At the age of 14 he began his apprenticeship in a Whitehaven shipyard and stayed there until finishing his time in 1769. At the age of 28 with a number of fellow shipbuilders, he emigrated to New England which was then under British rule; it was there in 1770 that he started in his shipbuilding enterprise.
However, and due to the Boston Tea Party, he and his friends were forced to leave in a hurry; their escape took place in one of Brocklebank's newly completed ships the ***Castor***. At the time of their hurried departure back to England, they regrettably had to leave all their belongings behind. Arriving back at his home town of Whitehaven in June 1775, Brocklebank resumed in the shipbuilding trade and eventually became a ship owner.
By 1795, Daniel Brocklebank owned 12 ships, but due to ill health he retired from business in 1800, and died the following year at the age of 60. Daniel Brocklebank had two sons and a daughter, and in 1806, five years after his death, his sons Thomas and John formed their own shipbuilding and shipping company. This was the firm which was one day to become the world renowned T&J Brocklebank of Liverpool. These brothers never married, and neither did they have any descendants. However, after having married Captain Wilson Fisher from Whitehaven, their sister Annie gave birth to Thomas Fisher. At a later date and due to marriage failure, Annie reverted to her maiden name. Her son was then known as Thomas Brocklebank and he was eventually to become the sole descendant of the Brocklebanks.
The best remembered ship of the company and the one that laid a solid foundation to its future, was the 514 ton full rigged ship ***Princess Charlotte.*** She'd been built at the Brocklebank Whitehaven yard, where English oak as well as coppering was used in her construction. Completed in 1815, the vessel sailed on her maiden voyage to the East Indies in January 1816. She had accommodation for a number of passengers and was able to carry 800 tons of cargo.
On her return passage to Liverpool in 1818, the ***Princess Charlotte*** inaugurated the link for Brocklebanks between India and the UK. That voyage which lasted two years and two months was such a financial success, that the Brocklebank brothers immediately built a sister ship from the same plans; this resulted in the ***Perseverance*** joining the company in

1819. To the Brocklebanks, it became apparent that there was more financial reward in ship owning than shipbuilding, and despite the fact they kept their Whitehaven yards, the brothers expanded their trade to India and the East Indies. In 1824 the following advertisement appeared in Myers Mercantile Advertiser.

For Calcutta

The Fine Ship *Perseverance*

Burthen per register 512 tons: sails remarkably fast; has superior accommodation for passengers and carries a surgeon; now lying in the Princes Dock. For freight or passage apply to T&J Brocklebank.

During their early years of ship owning, all the company apprentices and deck officers came from the Cumbria area. It was in effect a closed shop, and 'foreigners' were not invited to join the firm. However, with owning so many ships at a later date, Brocklebanks were forced to supplement the officer's ranks; there just wasn't enough captains, mates or apprentices from the area to man their ever growing fleet. In the early years, the company's headquarters were kept at Whitehaven where their yards were situated; their ships however, were all registered at Liverpool from where they sailed. In 1819 an office for the fledging firm was opened at 15 Exchange Buildings, Liverpool.
Thomas Brocklebank took charge of the office leaving his brother to superintend at the shipyard. By this time the company owned 14 sailing vessels. When the East India Company's monopoly was finally abolished in 1833, the Brocklebank brothers moved in fast to extend their trade from Bombay to Singapore, however it was Calcutta that was to be the jewel in their crown. The company's shipbuilding yards at Whitehaven closed in 1865; by this time however, the company owned 23 ships averaging 900 tons in size.

Above—Built ship rigged in 1874, the *Belfast's* first owners were T&J Brocklebank of Liverpool. It was company policy to give their ships Indian names, but in a special agreement with Harland & Wolff the builders, this ship was named after the city in which she was built. In 1901 she was sold to the Shaw Saville & Albion Line, and as the above picture shows, she was cut down to a barque rig. The *Belfast* went under Chilean ownership in 1906, then flew the American flag from 1916 onwards. In 1925 her last owner WR Grace laid her up at Norfolk Virginia.

HMS *Caronia*

A former Cunard liner converted to an Armed Merchant Cruiser. During WW1 she captured the *Odessa*, a vessel that was once the former Brocklebank ship *Holkar,* then with a boarding party sailed her into Falmouth.

Sindia

The T&J Brocklebank company continued to grow, and by the year 1887 they owned a large fleet of both sail and steam. In that year they took delivery of the four masted barque ***Sindia.*** When she came off the stocks, she was yet another ship that briefly held the record of being the world's largest merchant sailing ship. The ***Sindia*** had a length of 329.3 feet bp, a beam of over 45 feet, and a depth of hold of 26.7 feet, allowing her to carry 4,800 deadweight tons on a gross tonnage of 3,068. She had a poop-deck of 53 feet, and a foc'sle head of 35 feet; however, she was not built with the currently popular Liverpool House. Instead, the ship had three deckhouses, the most forward of which, was used as the sailor's foc'sle, the centre one for the idlers and galley, with the apprentices half deck in the after most house. The ship's hull was painted black, and the broad white line that ran from stem to stern was indeed a feature of all Brocklebank ships, even to the end of the twentieth century. Another item of interest was the company house flag, half blue and half white, the white half of the flag on the halyard. As Brocklebanks had become the oldest shipping company in the world, and as an unwritten mark of respect, they were the only company 'allowed' to fly their house-flag from the foremast. The ***Sindia's*** first few voyages were to India, often taking out coal or salt on her outward trips, then returning to the UK with jute, hides or linseed. She couldn't use the Suez Canal as would her contemporaries the steamers, and it wasn't long before she came off the route altogether to go on the grain run. This didn't work out too well either, and Brocklebanks who were by then totally committed to steam, decided to sell their remaining sailing vessels.

The ***Sindia*** was unwanted, and in 1899 she followed the route of so many other large ships of sail by going to the Anglo American Oil Company. Under her new owners, she began carrying case oil from New York to the Far East. Unfortunately, the new owners only had her for a couple of years before she came to a premature end. She had loaded a cargo of chrome ore and was bound from Kobe to New York when disaster struck. After having sailed halfway around the world and with just a few miles to go to her destination, the vessel was hit by a snow blizzard in December 1902. The big ship was driven onto a lee shore at Ocean Beach New Jersey and became stuck in the sand. The crew were saved, but despite all the attempts of the salvors, the big ship couldn't be towed back into the water. However, most of the cargo was taken off bit by bit at a later date. As time passed the 15 year old ship began to break up, but even after many years, the remains of ***Sindia*** could still be seen sticking up from out of the sand.

Sindia

From an oil painting by the author

Holkar

In the year of 1888, the ***Holkar*** became the last ever sailing vessel to be built for T&J Brocklebank; her tonnage and appearance were the same as the ***Sindia,*** and in her early years of trading, she followed the same route. The ***Holkar's*** rig was quite straightforward in having steel pole masts with wooden t'gallants. On her maiden voyage to India she was commanded by Captain Ellery; then on the vessel's return to Liverpool, Captain Ellery left the ***Holkar*** to take command of one of the company's new steamers. He was relieved by Captain W Peterkin who stayed with the ship until the turn of the century.

Holkar was sold to the German firm of DH Watjen in 1901. The four masted barque was renamed ***Adelaide*** and fitted with brace winches, she also adopted the familiar German style of double gaff sails on the jigger mast. The company used the ship on the Australian grain run, before she was sold to another German firm in 1913 and re-named ***Odessa.*** It was under that name however, and after making just one voyage for her new owner, that the First World War began.

After having loaded a general cargo in Hamburg and whilst outward bound down the English Channel, she was intercepted by the Armed Merchant Cruiser and former Cunard liner ***HMS Caronia*** in November 1914. The ***Odessa*** was sailed into Falmouth by a boarding party, her cargo was removed and confiscated by the British government.

Having no use for the vessel, the Admiralty sold the big barque sometime in 1915 to A Meling of Stavanger for £8,700; her name then changed to ***Souverain.*** From then on, she changed hands four times whilst under the Norwegian flag. Firstly she went to Tvedestrands Red Akt, and then in 1917 was sold to the Christiansand Shipping Co who kept her until 1920. She then went to the Skibs A\S Ostra, (Capt. Lars Jorgensen) and later still in 1922, her last owner Emil Knudsen of Lillesand bought the vessel and renamed her ***Hippalos***.

In 1924, the ***Hippolos*** arrived at Le Havre from Melbourne with a cargo of wheat. After an extremely long and hazardous passage, her crew were in bad shape suffering from beri beri. Besides this problem, she must have been a most uneconomical ship considering the number of owners she'd had. After the vessel had been laid up for a year at the French port, her owner was unable to secure a charter, a buyer or a crew. Laid up ships cost money, and whilst in a crew-less state old ships deteriorate rapidly. Moreover, the ***Hippolos*** was due for a survey. Therefore, Emil Knudsen sold the 36 year old veteran to a Dutch knacker's yard in 1925.

Under tow with two black balls showing on her forestay, the former Liverpool ship *Holkar* is seen here under the Norwegian flag as the *Hippalos*.
Her three lower yards are braced and canted, an indication that she may be going to use them as derricks whilst going alongside port side to the quay.

Mersey

James Nourse of London operated a large fleet of sailing vessels. His ships were all named after prominent rivers and one of them was the full rigged ship ***Mersey***. Whilst under the ownership of Nourse, the ship's livery was red boot topping, grey ship's side with a broad white band on which there were 14 painted gunports, all topped by a black bulwark and top rail. ***Mersey*** was built at the yard of Charles Connell on the Clyde in 1894, three masted and ship rigged, her polemasts and spike bowsprit made her a typical ship of the era. When first built, she registered 1,713 tons gross, her length was 270.7 feet, beam 39 feet and a moulded depth of 22.5 feet. The ***Mersey*** was a sister ship to the ***Forth,*** also owned by James Nourse. Most of her trading was to the far east, and while she was under the Nourse management she carried a large crew of Asians; the vessel was well maintained and always of pristine appearance.

In the year 1907 however, the ***Mersey*** was sold to the White Star Line of Liverpool, who, it may be said, would take exception to purchasing only the finest of ships. For the purpose of sail training, this company had recently operated the barque ***California,*** but after having sold her in 1895, the White Star Line thought they had dispensed with the idea of sail training altogether. However, it would appear that the idea of putting their midshipmen through those rigours had been resurrected; so once again the company's future officers were sent on a toughening up course. It then became company policy for all deck officers to have some experience in sail, even if it was regarded as a thing of the past.

Under her new ownership some changes were made, but the ship retained her original name of ***Mersey***. The skysail she carried on her mainmast was sent down, the mast re-headed, and reef points were added to the courses and upper topsails. The ship's side was then painted grey and accommodation made for 60 trainees with classrooms installed in the 'tweens. In her days as a general trader for Nourse, the ***Mersey*** carried a total complement of around 28, that figure was now increased to 102. The ***Mersey*** carried on where the ***California*** had left off; her route was the same as her predecessor in after having left Liverpool, she'd make a round the world voyage which took about 12 months. The voyage would take her to Brazil, River Plate, Cape of Good Hope, and Australia with general cargo, then around Cape Horn and back to Liverpool with grain or wool. As her captains were always Royal Naval reservists, the ***Mersey*** flew the blue ensign from her gaff. At the outset of the Great War in 1914, the company decided not to send such a large number of boys to sea for fear of enemy action. Having no other ships of sail, and no real interest in the future of sail, the ***Mersey*** was sold to the Transatlantic Shipping Co of Norway and re-named ***Transatlantic.***

Out came all the accommodation which had been installed to house the 60 cadets, the vessel was once again used for the purpose of carrying freight around the world. Not for long though, because in 1916 she changed hands to the Christiana School Ship Association. The ship was again to be used for sail training and the cadet accommodation was re-installed. Unfortunately for the School Ship Association, a new law was passed which did not permit the ship to put to sea with trainees during wartime, out came the accommodation and the ship was sold on yet again. In 1917 the ship's name changed to ***Dvergso,*** the new owners kept the veteran until 1922, before selling her to Lars Jorgensen. He didn't keep her long either, and after only a few months sold the little full rigger. The vessel which had been a first ship to so many of the White Star Line's deck officers then went to the breaker's yard.

In a letter to the Sea Breezes January 1951 issue, there was an interesting article written by R V Fry concerning the ship *Mersey;* a short part of his article is reproduced.

"I was in the ***Bardowie*** moored to two anchors in Montevideo, when one day we sighted a sail far out to sea. This proved to be the full rigged ship ***Mersey*** running free and straight for harbour. As she came on she clewed up furling her royals, double topgallants, and downed all her staysails. When she arrived near the entrance she clewed up the three courses and hauled down all the headsails; clewing up her fore topsails she dropped her port anchor, paid out cable freely and swung around. She squared the yards, came aback and let go her starboard anchor, clewed up the topsails, brailed in the spanker and hove in on the port cable to effect a 45 fathom mooring.

At that particular time the ***Mersey*** was the White Star Line training ship, and we were told the notorious 'Bullwanger Steel' was her chief officer. When she came into Montevideo, the weather was fine with a moderate breeze and she made a grand sight. I'd been working up in ***Bardowie's*** main t'gallant crosstrees and had a good view. I could see all the ships in harbour stopping work to watch the ***Mersey's*** fine feat of seamanship. She came in with a cargo of coal which we were also discharging. There were many sailing vessels in harbour at the time, nearest to us were the ships ***Vimeira,*** and ***Clyde,*** the four masted ship ***Lancing*** and the Bank Line's four masted barque ***Speke***

Author's Collection

Mersey

Gwydyr Castle

The steel three mast barque *Newfield* of 1,512 gross tons, was built in 1893 for Brownells of Liverpool by Stephen & Sons of Dundee. In 1898 she was sold to R Thomas & Co also of Liverpool and re-named *Gwydyr Castle.* The vessel traded worldwide during which time she paid many visits to the WCSA. One of her many crew members over the years was the noted German marine artist Anton Fischer, and it was while serving aboard the barque that he produced many a splendid painting. In 1916 the barque was sold to a Newfoundland company, then after the First World War went to an owner from Mauritius. After being laid up in 1925, the *Gwydyr Castle* was scrapped in 1932.

Eurasia

Seen in this picture with her royal sails on deck is the Liverpool registered *Eurasia.* Built by William Russell of Glasgow for Colonel Goffey in 1885, the 1,825 iron clipper was a sister ship to the *Malasia,* a ship that was lost with all hands when just a year old. *Eurasia's* first captain was William Parkes of Seaforth; he had the ship for seven years before being relieved by Captain Daniel Hughes. Captain Parkes then left to take command of *Austrasia* which was another of Goffey's ships. The first few trips of the *Eurasia* was to Australia, but afterwards she went on the Liverpool to San Francisco run. Sold to the Italians in 1909 she lasted until 1918, at that point with the war almost over, she was torpedoed by a German U boat.

Kate Thomas

The *Kate Thomas* was built in 1885 by William Doxford & Sons of Sunderland. She was one of three sister ships built to the order of William Thomas of Liverpool who ran a large fleet of sail. The other two vessels were the *Principality* and *Colony*. These three barques are said to be the smallest four masted barques ever built, but with their short lengths of 258 feet and 1,748 gross tons, they all gave good accounts of themselves with regards to speedy passages. They were all Cape Horners.

However, the *Kate Thomas* was noted for her two collisions more than anything else in her career, the first of which occurred during the summer of in 1906 off Beachy Head. This was when the much larger SS *Blanefield* misjudged the sailing vessels speed and collided with her, as a result the steamer sank.

The second collision happened when the *Kate Thomas* was under tow in ballast from Antwerp to Port Talbot. Apparently, there was a crew of seventeen plus both the captain's and first mate's wives aboard. The towing vessel's lights were bright as was her tow. However, in the darkness at the end of the middle watch on one April 1910 morning, the sailing vessel was suddenly smashed into by the steamer *India,* a vessel that was inward bound to Penzance. Despite the fact there were a number of the crew and the officer's wives alerted and up on deck, it would appear that because the *Kate Thomas* sank so quickly, there was not enough time to launch any of the lifeboats. Eventually there was only one survivor to tell the tale, an apprentice named Jack Nelson. In his statement he said he saw the SS *India* steam away after the collision, and the *Kate Thomas* took just eight minutes to go under.

Glossary

A

Aback-When the sails are blowing the opposite way to which they are intended
Abaft - Behind.
Able Seaman-A qualified first class seaman who is able to perform any job on deck.
Aloft - Up the mast.
Anchor gong - Operated from the foc'sle head, in conjunction with the foghorn from aft. A copper plate like object which when struck with a soft mallet, creates a warning sound to other ships in the fog.

B

Backsheesh– A handout or donation
Bald Header-A sailing vessel which has no sails above the upper t'gallants.
Ballast-Extra weight carried by an unladen ship to give it stability
Barque-A square rigged sailing vessel with at least three masts that is fore and aft rigged on its aftermost mast.
Barque Rigged - As above.
Barquentine– A fore and aft sailing vessel with at least three masts, which is square rigged on the foremast only.
Battened Down - Secured to be watertight.
Beam-The maximum width of a vessel's hull
Beam Ends-A ship is said to be on its beam ends when it has capsized and is laying on its side
Bearing - The angle from the ship to another object.
Beating or Beating to Windward - Sailing a ship into the wind.
Binnacle-The compass housing.
Bitts - A pair of steel cylindrical posts used for securing berthing ropes.
Blocks - Wooden or steel cheeks which hold a sheave for the running rigging.
Blue Peter - The P flag of the international code of signals, which when flown indicates that the ship is due to sail.
Boat Fall– A tackle used for lowering a lifeboat
Boot Topping-A specially painted band around the ship's hull below the waterline. Used especially to resist marine growth. Also a name for the brick red paint.
BP - An abbreviation for between perpendiculars. This is a length which is between the rabbet behind the ship's stem, to the inside of the stern frame on the main deck. The BP of a ship is its length.
Bosun - A shortened version of the word boatswain. The senior deck-hand.
Bowsed In - Rope in to stop unwanted movement.
Bowsprit-A spar that protrudes from the stem of a ship at a steved angle. It is used to support the stays and head-sails from the foremast, and a jib-boom if one is carried..
Bow-Bows-The flared forepart of the hull – the overhang of the foc'sle head.

Braces-Ropes secured to the end of the yardarms which are used to haul or swing theyards around
Brace Winch– A hand operated winch which hauls the braces.
Brick Dust - Ground brick made into a fine powder for polishing brass.
Bucko Mate - A name given to a first mate who physically bullied the sailors.
Bulkhead - A steel separating wall, termed usually as those between cargo holds, but any walling inside a ship's accommodation is referred to as a bulkhead.
.**Bulwark** - The wooden or steel wall on the upper deck which stops sailors from being washed overboard.
Bung- As used as a plug in the bottom of a life-boat
Bunkers - Engine fuel ie coal or oil
Bunt-The centre of the yard.
Buntlines-Ropes that are used to pull the foot of the sail up to the yard.
Burlap - Sacking material.

C

Cable-The anchor chain.—As a length, one cable is equal to 100 fathoms or 600 feet.
Careen-When a ship is hove down in the shallows to have her bottom scraped and painted.
Case Oil– Two five gallon drums of oil packed into a wooden box.
Ceylon - Now known as Sri Lanks.
Chain Plate– Fastenings on the ship's side below the channels that take the weight and strain of the shrouds and backstays.
Chain Sling-A heavy iron chain that takes the weight of the lower yard at the bunt.
Channels– Channels is a word derived from Chain Whales. These are platforms which are built into and onto the ship's side adjacent to each mast on both sides. Their purpose is to provide the shrouds and backstays with a securing point, thus giving a better radius for increased stability of the masts. With the advent of wire rope they became obsolete.
Clewed-When the lower corners of a sail are hauled up to the yard.
Chippy - The ship's carpenter.
Clipper Ship-Slang word for a ship built for speed that has fine under water lines.
Coaming - A buffer plate 0f about one foot in height situated at a doorway to stop sea-water entering the accommodation. Also used at a cargo hatch.
Companionway - A railed ladder leading to the next deck below.
Compass Card - The circular card inside the magnetic compass, on which the points of the compass or degrees are printed
Coppered-A wooden hulled ship is said to be coppered when its underwater has been sheathed with copper plates which protects it from worm and other unwanted growth
Course– The direction in which a ship is travelling.
Counter Stern - A ship's stern designed to counter following seas boarding the ship.
Course– The large lower sail of each mast. **Also -** the compass direction of a ship.
Crab Winch– A capstan like device through which a rope passes when being hauled. The rope can be stoppered off with the use of a screw press.
Crimps-Unlawful people who traded in the sale of seamen to undermanned ships.
Cut Down-A ship is said to be cut down when its rig is reduced. ie; from ship to barque

D

Davit - ie Radial Davit. For use when lifting a boat from its chocks and swinging it over the side.
Dead Horse-After receiving a month's advance of wages on joining his ship, a sailor's first month on board was known as flogging a dead horse.
Deadweight-See tonnages.
Derrick. A swinging steel cylindrical boom which acts as a crane.
Doldrums-Windless zones.
Donkey-man The senior engine room rating under the engineers.
Donkey's Breakfast - A name given to a straw filled mattress on which the sailors slept.
Dolly Winch A hand winch generally used for cargo.
Down Helm - An order from captain to helmsman to slack off the wheel.
Dunnage - Waste wood planks -generally used in the cargo holds for layering or spacing between differing types of cargo.

E

Eight Bells-The number of bell rung at midnight, 4 am, 8 am, noon, 4 pm, and 8 pm.

F

Fathom-A nautical measurement which is equal to six feet or two yards.
Fidley - The engine room skylight of a steamer.
Flogging a Dead Horse - When seamen were given a month's advance of wages on joining their ship, the first month at sea was to work their debt off. This was known as 'Flogging a Dead Horse.'
Foghorn - Used in conjunction with the anchor gong an implement which when wound up, creates a warning noise to other ships.
Forrard– The forward part of the ship.
Foc'sle-Accommodation for the sailors in whatever part of the ship it may be.
Foc'sle Head-Abbreviation for Fore Castle Head. The anchor deck in the forepart of the ship. The name originates from the early Men O' War where the ship's soldiers and marines would position themselves for battle.
Freeing Ports - Lids in the bulwarks which swing open with the roll of the ship, in turn this allows the water to run off the deck and back overboard.
Futtock Shrouds– The three short shrouds that run at an approximate angle of 45% from the top of the lower mast shrouds, through to the lower mast table via the lubber's hole. Their purpose is to assist in holding down the topmast.

G

Galley-A ship's kitchen.
Galley Wireless - Nothing to do with a galley or a wireless, but a source of from where rumours and gossip emanate.
Gash Bucket - A bucket used in the galley or mess-room for waste.
Gear– Any moveable item on board - often referred to as clothing.

H

Half-deck-Accommodation for the apprentices.
Halyard - Originally known as a 'haul yard.' Ropes that hoist a yard to its position. Also a name given to the line which hoists flags.
Hard Tack - Ship's biscuit. Once a meal but latterly used as lifeboat victuals.
Harness Cask-Oaken barrels used for storing meat in brine.
Harriet Lane– Tinned meat; its name originating from a lady who disappeared whilst working in a meat canning factory in London.
Hawse Pipe - The aperture from the foc'sle head to ship's side through which the anchor shank is held on modern steamers, and where the anchor cable runs out from the chain locker.
Heads - The sailor's latrine.
Heeled - When a ship is purposefully sailing at a designed angle.
High and Dry - When a ship has been beached.
Helm - The ship's steering wheel.
Hook-A slang name given to a ship's anchor.
Hogging– When a ship is lifted by a big sea amidships causing strain on the hull. Ships can also hog after having run aground.
Holystoning - The barbarising and cleaning of wooden decks with the use of a type of sandstone.
Homeward Bounder - A ship which is heading towards her home country. Also a derogatory name given to somebody who stitches canvas or material poorly.
House Flag - A flag which is flown to identify the ship's owner.
Hows your head?- A question from the officer of the watch to the helmsman, asking him to give the compass reading at that exact time.
Hull-The main body of a ship.
Hull Down - When just the sails or superstructure of a ship are visible on the horizon.

I

Idlers - The dayworkers who consist of the bosun, cook carpenter, sailmaker and steward.

J

Jib-Boom-An extension to the bowsprit.
Jib Sheets - The ropes that control the jib sails.
Jigger - The fourth mast from forward.

K

Kedge Anchor-A smaller anchor used for stern mooring.
Keel-The backbone and main support of a ship's hull.
Knots - As well as bends and hitches, this was a term given to the speed of the ship. A nautical mile is 6,080 feet whilst a land mile is 5.760 feet.

L

Larrikin-Australian or New Zealand slang for a hooligan.
Lazarette-A small hatched space used for ship's stores or equipment, not a cargo space.
Lee-rail-The bulwark top on the side away from the weather.
Life-line-A rope set up on the main deck used for sailors to hold onto in heavy weather.
Light weather Sails - Older or patched sails used in light weather conditions.
Lime Juicer-A British ship.
Liverpool House-A raised deck house amidships that covers the beam of the ship.

Log - The book in which all instances and actions are recorded on a ship.
Logged-Entered in the ship's log book. Other - A seaman who is fined for an offence.
Long Splice-A splice made in either cordage or wire rope which allows that part of the rope to pass through a sheaved block.
Lubbers Hole - The aperture in the mast table through which the futtock shrouds pass.

M

Mainsail Haul - An order given by the captain to his crew when tacking ship.
Mercantile Marine-Otherwise referred to as the Merchant Navy
Made Masts-Manufactured masts ie; The lower mast requirements of some wooden ships were often so large in length and circumference, that they had to be made up in sections then banded together.
Master-The captain - also referred to as 'the Old Man.'
Mate-The chief deck officer or first mate.
Mate's Ticket-A mate's certificate of competency.
Middle-watch The deck watch between midnight and four am.
Midshipman-A future officer in training.
Mizzen - The third mast from forward.
Muffled Oars– Boat oars with cloth wrapped around the oar's loom to make a silent approach.

N

Nautical Mile-A nautical mile measures 6,080 feet—a land mile is 5,760.
No Bottom-A call by the leadsman who in taking soundings can not take a reading.
Nett Tons– See Tonnages.
Norwegian Steam-Muscle power, or brute strength.

O

Old Man - The captain.
Over the Wall. - Over the side.

P

Packet or Packet Ship-A passenger ship.
Pampero-A River Plate Hurricane.
Pantile - Extremely hard ship biscuit made in the galley.
Passage-When a ship is sailing from one port to its next.
Pier Head Jump-Sailors who join the ship at the last minute.
Pier Head Artist-A marine artist who has never served at sea.
Pinnace - A small vessel used as a ferry.
Point - As a 360 degree circle is divided into 32 parts of eleven and one quarter degrees, they are known as points of the compass.
Poop Deck-A raised structure at the after end of the ship. Originally this was the latrine deck where a large box was hung over the stern for use as the officer's toilet.
Porridge Gannet - A name given to a Scotsman who has a ravenous appetite.

Q

Quarter - That part of the ship which is right aft.
Quarter Deck - The deck on the aftermost part of a ship.
Quarter Point, One quarter of one point of the compass. There are 128 quarter points on the compass.

R

Rain Sail-A spare canvas or old sail used to catch water in rain downpours.
Ratlines - Short lengths of line which pass across the lower shrouds to form a ladder for going aloft.
Ready about - An order from the captain of a sailing ship when tacking ship.
Rigging - The running and standing ropes and wires which support the masts and control the sails.
Roband - A short length of rope yarn which can have many purposes.
Rovings - Short lengths of rope yarns used for securing the head of a sail to the jack-stay on a yard arm.
Rubble-Ballast such as sand, stones or shale.
Runner-A disreputable person who works for a crimp.
Running Rigging-Ropes that run freely through sheaved blocks or deadeyes to control the sails or other.

S

Sag-Sagging-When a ship is strained amidships by being lifted by its fore and after ends in big seas. See Hogging.
Sailmaker - The seaman who makes and repairs a ship's sails.
Saloon - Officers dining room.
Servings - Tarred hemp or seizing wire wound tightly around a larger rope with a serving mallet to prevent chafing.
Schooner - A fore and aft sailing vessel.

Schooner Rigged-Besides being a rig name for a fore and aft sailing vessel, it is also a derogatory name given to a seaman who is short of clothing or other means.
Scuttle– to purposefully sink a vessel. Also a word for port-hole.
Shackle of Cable-A length of fifteen fathoms or ninety feet that is usually associated with anchor cables.
Shanghaied. Forcibly made or tricked into joining a ship.
Scupper - A drain or waterway as in a kitchen sink.
Scuppered - A ship which has been purposefully sunk.
Shanty - or Chanty - A sailor's song often used whilst working to keep up momentum and spirits.
Sheer Pole-The bar that runs along the bottom of shrouds to keep them evenly balanced.
Ship-A sailing vessel with at least three masts that is square rigged on all masts, but has a spanker sail on the most after mast.
Ship Rigged - As above.
Shrouds-Heavy ropes that support the lower mast.
Skinned Out-Or backed out. A slang word for deserting a ship.
Smoko - Tea or coffee break.
Soojied - The washing of paint work
Spanker - The fore and aft sail on the aftermost mast of a square rigger.
Splice-The joining together of two ropes in either a cut, long or short splice; or the forming of an eye at one end of a rope.
Spoken - A ship is said to have been spoken when it exchanges signals with another vessel when at sea.
Square rigger - A sailing vessel which has its sails set at a ninety degree angle to the fore and aft line.
Standing Rigging-See shrouds.
Stay sails - The fore and aft sails that are situated in the fore and aft stays.
"Steady as she goes" An order from the officer of the watch to the helmsman, that he is to maintain the compass course shown at that exact moment.
Stern - The after end of a ship.
Stoke Hold - An engine room compartment where the fires for raising and maintaining steam is situated.
Stow Away - To store away until required.
Sub - An advance of wages.
Swallow the Anchor - A sailor is said to have swallowed the anchor when he has retired from sea life.
Sweating up a Rope-Heaving on a rope.
Swifter. As in shrouds; on every fifth ratline, a bar similar to a sheer-pole traverses the shrouds to keep them evenly balan

T

Tack– To zig-zag a ship through a headwind with the use of sails.
Taffrail - The safety rail which goes around the stern on the poop deck.
Taken Aback - When the wind suddenly comes from ahead causing the sails to blow the wrong way.
The Line - The equator
Thwart-A bench of a boat on which an oarsman sits

T'gallant-The mast above the topmast.
Tonnages-Ships are measured in different tonnages; The Gross Tonnage of a ship is measured on its cubic capacity ie; every 100 cubic feet equals one ton. Nett Tonnage is the same, less any spaces or compartments used for engine rooms, accommodation, store-rooms or any other space not used for cargo. Deadweight Tonnage is the weight of a ship's cargo. Displacement Tonnage is used by warships and is measured on the amount of water the ship displaces.
Travellers - Hoops that encircle the mast to which fore and aft sails are secured for their raising and lowering.
Truck - the round plate shaped object at the extreme top of each mast.
Turn To - Begin work.
'Tween Deck-A 'between' deck that is below the main deck.

U

U-Boat - A German submarine.
Up Helm - An order from captain to helmsman to bring the wheel up.

V

Vittles-Victuals.

W

Walkers Patent Log- An instrument that is trailed astern to measure the distance a ship has travelled.
Warped alongside - To maneouver a ship a ship into a berth, or move it further up or down the quay with the use of the ship's mooring ropes.
Watch your Head - An warning order from the officer of the watch to the helmsman . Usually when he is drifting off his course.
WCSA-West Coast of South America.
Weather Side - That part of the ship which catches the wind.
Whack. A sailor's ration of victuals.
Whaleback Stern-The rounded part of a ship's stern that leads from both quarters of the poop deck.
Windjammer-A slang word for a sailing vessel.**Yard**-A boom or spar that crosses the mast and is used for supporting a sail.

Y

Yankee Clipper-A name given to American built clippers for their Liverpool owner
Yards - The booms that run athwartships to the mast which hold the sails.
Yawing - When a ship slews from side to side in a seaway.

Sources of Information Bibliography and Publications

Argus - Cape Town.
A Sailors Scrapbook - G Belton - Square Sail Publishing. Cape Town.
Boulanger - Patrick - Chambre de Commerce Marseilles.
Cape Archives - Cape Town.
Cape Times - Cape Town.
Cape Town Maritime Museum.
Champion of Sail - D Walker - Conway Press.
Cornwall Advertiser.
Cubbin - Captain Graeme of T&J Harrison Lines
Dammerill - Wm of the *Lawhill* 1946.
Engstrande Hasse of Stockholm.
Gibson - Frank, St. Marys Scilly Isles.
Gibson - Sandra, St. Marys Scilly Isles.
Haggies- Steel Wire Ropes - South Africa.
Harris - Captain C J South African Navy.
Hogan - Dallas - Carrington, Newcastle NSW.
Jones - Mrs Bertha - Grand daughter of Captain Matthew Jackson of the *Halewood*.
Jones - Trevor and Glynn of J P Lamb, Liverpool ship chandlers.
Kay - Captain Joseph, of Shetland Isles - Grandson of Captain Thomas Kay of the *Criffel.*
Kinghorn - Captain AW of North Shields.
Les Derniers Cap Horniers Francaise - Louis Lacroix - Marseilles.
Liverpool County Museum.
Liverpool Echo
McIntyre - Gillian - Proof reading.
Marseille Maritime Museum.
Merseyside Maritime Museum.
Maguire - James - Carrington, Newcastle NSW.
Maritime South Africa - B Ingpen & Pabst - Janes Publishing Co Cape Town.
Meyer - Captain Keith - South African Navy.
Nankin - Phillip - First Mate of *Lawhill* 1946.
Netterburg - Captain Jack, South African Navy, formerly an AB of the *Parma.*
Newcastle NSW Maritime Museum.
Oslo Maritime Museum.
Penso - Victor, supernumary of *Lawhill* 1946
Penso Mrs R - Fishoek, South Africa.
Read - Gordon of the Liverpool County Museum.
Robinson R. Compass Adjusters, Hamble
Sea Breezes Magazine.
Ship's Monthly Magazine.
Smyth - Mrs Antoinette of Bideford - French Translations.
Spencer - Josh – Cape Town
Square Sail Publishing Cape Town.
Sweeney - Miss D - Dundee City Council.
Sydney Morning Herald.

Acknowledgements

Sydney Morning Herald
The Sun - Sydney.
The Courier and Advertiser - Dundee.
Taylor - Lucy, Churchwarden, St. Levans, Penzance.
The Authors Society, London.
The Last of the Windjammers Vol 1 and 2 Lubbock - Brown Son & Ferguson.
The Way of a Ship - Villiers - Hodder Stoughton.
The Nitrate Clippers - Lubbock - Brown Son & Ferguson.
The Passage Makers - Michael Stammers - Conway Press.
The Wanderer of Liverpool - John Masefield - Heineman Press.
The Windjammer Story - Villiers - Scholastic Books New York.
Western Port Wrecks and Mishaps - Arthur E Woodley - Newcastle NSW.
Wong - Mark Liverpool Retired Seamen's Institute..

Due to a lifetime of collecting pictures and stories for this and other publications, a period in which the author has amassed many thousands of oddments of text, postcards and photographs, every effort has been made to acknowledge the originators of those items, as well as those who have assisted in the making of this book. On advertising in 'Ship's Monthly' some years ago, for additional information and photographs for the 'Liverpool Windjammers' a tremendous response was received from all parts of the world. Therefore I am most grateful to those whose names are listed in the acknowledgements page, people whose contributions are alongside their name. However, if there is any text or photographs which have unknowingly been printed without an owner or an unknown copyright holder's consent, or indeed, if there are any mistakes within the text or photographs, then the author makes a full apology. If any person has any just or valid objection to any text or photographs within this book, it will be removed on the next edition.

INDEX